Lock, Stock, & Barrel

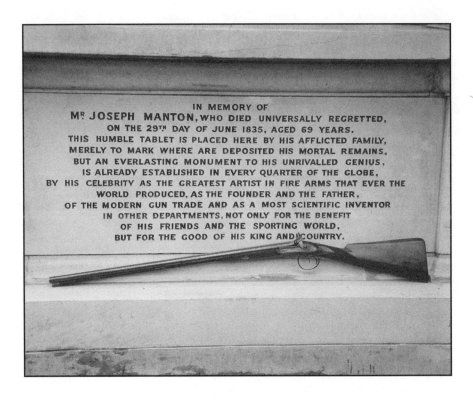

IN MEMORY OF
Mʀ JOSEPH MANTON, WHO DIED UNIVERSALLY REGRETTED,
ON THE 29ᵀᴴ DAY OF JUNE 1835, AGED 69 YEARS.
THIS HUMBLE TABLET IS PLACED HERE BY HIS AFFLICTED FAMILY,
MERELY TO MARK WHERE ARE DEPOSITED HIS MORTAL REMAINS,
BUT AN EVERLASTING MONUMENT TO HIS UNRIVALLED GENIUS,
IS ALREADY ESTABLISHED IN EVERY QUARTER OF THE GLOBE,
BY HIS CELEBRITY AS THE GREATEST ARTIST IN FIRE ARMS THAT EVER THE
WORLD PRODUCED, AS THE FOUNDER AND THE FATHER,
OF THE MODERN GUN TRADE AND AS A MOST SCIENTIFIC INVENTOR
IN OTHER DEPARTMENTS, NOT ONLY FOR THE BENEFIT
OF HIS FRIENDS AND THE SPORTING WORLD,
BUT FOR THE GOOD OF HIS KING AND COUNTRY.

Dedication

This book is dedicated to Joseph Manton, the father of the modern gun, and to the legion of skilled English gunmakers and craftsmen who succeeded him. They have left us with a legacy of the finest sporting guns ever produced. May we treat these guns with deserving respect and shoot them with competence.

Lock, Stock, & Barrel

Making an English shotgun and shooting with consistency

by

Cyril S. Adams &
Robert S. Braden

Safari Press, Inc.

Adams, Cyril S.
Braden, Robert S.

Second edition.

ISBN 1-57157-020-9

Library of Congress Catalog Card Number: 95-72214

10 9 8 7 6 5 4 3 2

1996, Long Beach, California, USA

Readers wishing to receive the Safari Press catalog, featuring many fine books on big-game hunting, wingshooting, and firearms, should write the publisher at the address given above.

This is the 65th book published by Safari Press.

Table of Contents

Foreword

For a couple of Americans setting out to do a definitive book on fine English shotguns, Cyril Adams and Bob Braden share a relatively rare qualification. They know what they're talking about. I can say that with conviction, having done a great deal of shooting research of my own and having hunted birds with them, shared shotgun studies, debated double guns, and shot clays with them for more than twenty-five years.

It was, in fact, about thirty years ago, at the old Greater Houston (Texas) Gun Club that I noticed a tall fellow stepping out onto the long yardage handicap line. He was at the box pigeon ring and he cradled a beautiful old Damascus-barreled English hammer gun. He shot the gun the way fine guns should be shot. He cocked the hammers without looking at them, and when the bird appeared, it dropped instantly in successive puffs of feathers. The old gun's double triggers had been strummed so smoothly that the two barrels spoke almost as one.

That was Cyril Adams. I've since seen him take many a bird, including enough clay ones to win the Texas State Sporting Clays championship and numerous helice (ZZ) competitions with his favorite London best Grant hammer gun made in about 1890. I always thought he was simply accepting a handicap with that old gun, perhaps for reasons of nostalgia or its elegance. Then one day he let me shoot it. This thing of grace and beauty turned out to have a life of its own. It literally moved after targets as if it were self-willed rather than being pushed.

Since then I've paid a lot more attention to what Adams says about shotguns. His knowledge of English guns is so profound, yet common sense practical, that many times I have relied on his answers to questions from my readers rather than delving into definitive books by English authorities. One reason is that his knowledge is not just academic. He's still sufficiently involved with the English gun trade that he maintains a flat in London.

It was during a south Texas dove shoot that I really got to know Braden. We were shooting some distance from each other, and we gradually worked nearer to one another. We each wanted to observe how the other was making some of those long shots. Not only was I impressed by his technique, but also by his intelligence and inquisitive nature in discussing differences in our styles. I've since learned that I'd have been better off paying more attention to his English shooting-schooled techniques then, rather than having to develop them later in order to win at sporting clays.

Braden is a consummate student of detail in whatever he does. He is a highly-successful businessman. He brings to this book his gleanings from shooting and studying shooting around the world. Both Braden and Adams tell it as they see it, and often with humor. Braden, for example, once mentioned to me that God shoots an English hammer gun. Once, when I asked Adams his opinion of a certain over/under with twenty-six-inch barrels, he said it was probably a pretty good gun for holding up convenience stores.

There are a few points made in this book with which I cannot agree, which is to be expected when any three students of the shotgun compare notes and experiences. For any shooter or hunter serious about fine English guns, or anyone interested in an informative distillation of shooting tips from the cream of the crop of British instructors, this will be a book referred to many times after its original reading. It's absorbing, and it treats the best gun as it should be treated, not just as a tool, but as a pleasure.

Bob Brister
Shooting Editor, *Field & Stream*

Preface

Friendships are often born of unusual circumstances. We came to know one another over thirty years ago in the border town of Eagle Pass, between Texas and Mexico. We accidentally crossed paths in pursuit of that challenging game bird, the mourning dove. Considering our mutual passion for wing shooting and our common educational backgrounds in civil engineering, a lasting friendship was virtually assured. Over the next several years, we also decided to expand our horizons.

Since this first casual meeting in south Texas, we have shot birds in sixteen countries that span four continents. We have also exposed ourselves to some of the finest wing shooters of the second half of this century, have competed more or less successfully with them, and have learned much from superb shooting instructors in Britain and America. During the course of our odyssey, we have tried every type of shotgun produced from the 1860s to the present.

Our journey was so fascinating that Adams abandoned a sensible engineering practice to earn his way in the world as a gun dealer. Fortunately, the engineer in him demanded that he uncover each component that goes into making a great shotgun. This pursuit led him to gun factories throughout the world, to seductive, detailed meetings with individual masters of the art of gunmaking, to in-depth research of the literature, to learning the sometimes difficult lessons of the gun trade, and ultimately to the challenge of making best guns.

Braden remained committed to shooting. He followed the more conventional pathway of learning about guns by the way they felt and pointed. In the process, he developed an enduring love for the shooting stage, for the backdrop of the field, and for the essence of what it all means to a sportsman.

These lifetime investments have led to a fair understanding of shooting and of the tools of the trade. Readers of *Lock, Stock, & Barrel* will become aware of our strong, collective bias regarding English shotguns and how to use them; we are unabashed in our opinions. Some shooters may not agree with what we say, but readers may have confidence these viewpoints are based on ninety years of combined, extensive experience and study. If we have strayed off target, it is not because *we haven't been there.*

The book is presented in two parts, covering subjects that are related only by the common thread of the gun itself. The purpose of "Part I – The English Shotgun" is to present an overview of these remarkable guns as the pinnacle of shotgun perfection, and why they deserve the reputation they enjoy. In "Part II – Shooting with Consistency," the authors have attempted to convey some of the lessons learned through great effort and from shooting hundreds of thousands of cartridges in practice and in the field.

We are obligated to far more mentors than we can name and to countless friends who have shared our experiences. It is our hope that this book, as a legacy of what has been a major part of our lives, will benefit those who read it.

Cyril S. Adams
Robert S. Braden

March, 1996

Acknowledgments

We owe much to the many gunsmiths whose workshops and stores we have visited over the years. We are also indebted to the many matches and schools where we picked up valuable bits of shooting advice along the way. The gradual accretion of this information over the years has been reinforced through personal experience and is reflected in this book. We are grateful to all those many persons who cast light on these subjects.

While it is virtually impossible to remember all the individuals who have passed along gems of information during our lifetime of investigation, it is fitting that special recognition be given those individuals whose contributions were of greatest value to us. We appreciated their gracious and unselfish input at the time it was given and we are forever in their debt because of its enduring quality.

Part I deals with technical and historical aspects of shotguns. We are particularly grateful to Ludwig Borovnik, Gordon Brent, Jess Briley, Bob Brister, George Caswell, Ivo Fabbri, Billy Hodge, Harry Lawrence, John Rowe, Ron Solari, Joe Toot, Mr. Verees, and David Winks for their contributions to our knowledge in this area. For information on shooting in Part II, we are indebted to Norman Clark, Ken Davies, Rudy Etchen, Rex Gage, Jay Herbert, Grant Ilseng, Patrick Lynch, David Olive, Chris Potter, Billy Purdue, Alan Rose, and Michael Rose.

We also gratefully acknowledge the assistance and advice of Barrett Allison, Robert Griffin, Bob McBee, Chris Potter, and Ron Solari, who read the manuscript and offered helpful comments and suggestions. Lieber Laboratories in Houston, particularly Butch Lieber, was most generous in allowing us the use of its studio facilities and in giving us technical support in producing most of the photographs in this book.

Finally, we are indebted to the authors whose printed works are listed in the two selected bibliographies included at the conclusion of this work. Fortunately, their valuable contributions are still available to all of us.

Part I

The English Shotgun

An Overview

Introduction to Part I

Guns discussed and pictured in "Part I – The English Shotgun" are all double-barreled. The vast majority of text deals with the side-by-side double. These elegant pieces are, with almost no dissent, considered to be the finest shotguns ever made. Frequent references will be made to best guns. This term in Britain has a special connotation, meaning the *crême de la crême,* the very best, the absolute top of the line.

A voluminous body of literature deals with the subject of the English shotgun, as is evident in part by the selected bibliographies included in this book. It is a history of progressive development over more than two centuries. It is a mechanical evolution, complete with its own natural selection process, which has led to the renowned best guns of Britain. It is also a story of individual craftsmen, of functional excellence, and of aesthetics.

Much of the literature on the English shotgun consists of narrative accounts of many systems that were tried, and the successes, failures, and tortuous process of trial and error. Some of these accounts are very well done. Others, while informative, have appeal only to dedicated students of the subject. It is a kindness to say that still others are boring, devastatingly so.

This presentation attempts to reduce volumes of available material to an overview of the English shotgun, with sufficient photographs to keep the narrative description within the bounds of reason. The objective, then, is readability at the sacrifice of detailed coverage, which is a delicate and dangerous trade-off. Some omissions, therefore, are inevitable.

Most shooters are aware that English guns are highly regarded but woefully expensive to own. Those shooters who have had actual exposure to these remarkable firearms share an enhanced appreciation of their merit. Surprisingly, however, very few people outside Britain have a full understanding of how these guns came to be, why the reputation for excellence is deserved, and why their cost is so high. Answering these questions is a primary purpose of this overview.

Any account of the English shotgun must include some history and tradition, otherwise it would be impossible to understand such terms as London best. In this day of modern manufacturing processes, it is difficult to accept that a working and durable mechanical product is actually a work of art as well. In chapters that follow, this theme is defined and explored.

Readers should bear in mind that the individually crafted London best shotguns were made with ghosts of such legends as the incomparable Joseph Manton and the likes of Boss, Grant, the Purdeys, and Woodward looking over the shoulders of the artisans who produced them. This is the story of British tradition at its best and of guns with quality and performance that is unexcelled.

✜ Chapter 1 ✜

Chronology

Whose distant footsteps echo
Throughout the corridors of Time.

– Henry Wadsworth Longfellow

Historical Context

It is essential in understanding the modern gun to know the development of the English shotgun from its earlier forms. The modern gun has, without question, evolved over the course of time. Sometime during the early 1600s, the French began to shoot flying birds. At the time, they used clumsily stocked, long, single-barrel guns and slow-burning, charcoal-based black powder. During Cromwell's hegemony, King Charles II spent much of his time in exile on the Continent and had been exposed to this new sport. Upon his return in 1660 to England and the throne, he introduced the concept to the British Isles and thereby initiated the process of gun development.

It was not until the latter part of the eighteenth century, however, that the technologies of gunmaking and gunpowder produced a practical shooting application. Reliable Damascus shotgun barrels came on the scene about 1770. By 1790, the flintlock was perfected and shootable double-barrel guns were introduced.

The acknowledged "father of the modern gun," Joseph Manton (1766-1835), put in motion the many advancements that took place in the middle of the nineteenth century. Remarkably, the last major development of the modern shotgun took place in 1909, when Boss perfected the over/under. Only refinements have marked the past eighty-five years, unless mass-produced, repeating shotguns and lesser quality double barrels are recognized as advancements.

The chronological charts that follow demonstrate some interesting, but little-known facts. For example, the flintlock era endured for about 170 years, as compared to only 125 years for current center-fire guns.

Muzzleloaders prevailed for 210 years, modern hammer guns for only about twenty years, and the hammerless ejectors of today have been available for the past 105 years.

Most mechanical features of the modern gun came into existence during an amazingly productive period from 1850 to 1910. The new innovations were vigorously debated by shooters and makers alike. It was a period when percussion, pinfire and center-fire guns could all be seen in action on shooting estates. It was the practice of London's famous *Field* magazine to sponsor field trials from time to time (see "Chronology of Major Events" chart) to test the effectiveness of the new concepts.

In one sense, the story of shotgun development is a paradigm of the Industrial Revolution, but it is a contradiction as well. The best of English shotguns were not mass produced. Instead, they endured as a mechanical art form. Great craftsmen with skilled hands continued to produce them, and no doubt Joseph Manton would have been proud of the fine guns his successors made.

Chronological Charts

The summary chart that follows is based on dates taken from extensive gun literature covering this early period. The selected bibliography presented at the conclusion suggests sources for further reference.

DATES OF GENERAL INTEREST IN THE
CHRONOLOGY OF SHOOTING FLYING TARGETS

1660 Early British wing shooting (approximate)	**Flintlock Era** **170 Years**	
		Muzzleloaders **210 Years**
1770 Damascus barrels perfected (approximate)		
1790 Flintlock perfected; double-barrel guns		
1807 Percussion ignition		
1820 Percussion cap perfected		
	Percussion Era **40 Years**	
1846 Pinfire		
1861 Center-fire		
1870 Breechloader perfected		**Hammer Guns 20 Years**
1875 Choke perfected		
1880 Hammerless guns perfected; steel barrels	**Center-fire Era** **125 Years**	
1890 Smokeless powder; ejectors perfected		**Hammerless Ejectors** **105 Years**
1909 Over/under guns		
1995		

CHRONOLOGY OF MAJOR EVENTS IN DEVELOPMENT OF THE ENGLISH SHOTGUN
1800 to 1910

1807	Forsyth Percussion Priming	
1843	LeFaucheux Breechloader (France; approx.)	
1851	London Crystal Palace Exhibition Pin-fire Cartridges; Drop Down Barrels	
1858		***Major London "Field" Trial
1859	Jones Underlever	***Major London "Field" Trial
1861	Daw Center-fire Cartridge	
1862	Westley Richards Sliding Top Lever; Smokeless Powder	
1863	Purdey Sliding Bolt	
1865	Scott Spindle	
1866	Pape Choke	***Major London "Field" Trial
1867	Stanton Rebounding Lock; Greener Cross Bolt	
1874	Needham Ejector; Barrel Cocking	
1875	Anson & Deeley Boxlock	***Major London "Field" Trial
1878	Purdey Concealed Third Bite	***Major London "Field" Trial
1879	Rigby & Bissel Rising Bite	
1880	Beesley Self-opening Action	
1887	Holland Safety Sidelock	
1889	Southgate Ejector	
1897	Woodward and Holland Single Trigger	
1909	Boss Over/Under	

✤ Chapter 2 ✤

Barrels

The English maker takes a barrel that will do best; the foreign maker the barrel that will look best.

– W. W. Greener

Background and Development

Which of the essential components lock, stock, or barrel is the heartbeat of the total gun? A strong contingent of experts would insist that barrels are the most important. This position has many supportable arguments. A shotgun, for whatever else commends it, has no value without a finely bored, well-balanced set of barrels. Barrels, after all, contribute vitally to a smooth swing and accurate point, and at the same time safely project and shape the shot charge.

Direct antecedents of modern barrels were perfected in the late 1700s. Except for absence of choke boring, the balance and beauty of Joseph Manton's masterful Damascus flintlock guns of circa 1790 compare with the best quality of guns produced in our own time. Many of the famous, or favorite, sets of barrels from muzzleloading flintlocks were converted in the early 1800s to percussion guns. This was achieved by fitting them with a new breech and remaking the locks. Some percussion barrels were so highly regarded that they were converted to pinfire or center-fire by an expensive addition of a break-open action, new locks, and a new stock.

Because early barrel makers did not have access to improved metallurgy that came about just before the turn of the twentieth century, and because the machine technology of boring a straight hole thirty-six inches long was also not available, these pioneering practitioners found it necessary to employ difficult techniques to achieve strength, durability, and weight in their barrels. It is hard to imagine the skill required to make light, thin-walled (0.030-inch) barrels capable of withstanding the pressure of firing under the technologically primitive circumstances of the day. The barrels were the approximate thickness of a modern credit card.

These early shotgun barrels were made by using hard, low-carbon steel and soft, low-carbon iron in a unique combination that enabled the finished barrel to be hard enough to avoid bulging and denting, yet elastic enough to restore itself to proper size after the pressure wave passed. The process of producing Damascus barrels was remarkable in itself. By about 1875, when requirements of choke boring added another level of stress, lesser quality barrels could not be used for best guns. English Damascus barrel makers continued to improve the quality of their product until it met the new demands. The reputations of barrel makers rose, and today these great artisans enjoy prominence even in this period of steel barrel making.

The Damascus Misconception

Shotgun barrels were first made by rolling up the edges of a long, flat piece of low-carbon plate around a mandrel, and then forge welding the longitudinal seam. Some of the results were good, but this procedure had the inherent weakness of an extended seam along the entire length of barrel. Because it was subjected to the full load of hoop stress, the pressure wave from firing tended to split the longitudinal seam.

In the late 1700s, some ingenious craftsman, inspired by a common sense understanding of these forces, determined that a near 90-degree rotation of the seam would better accommodate the hoop stress effect. Rotation was achieved by winding thin strips of material around the

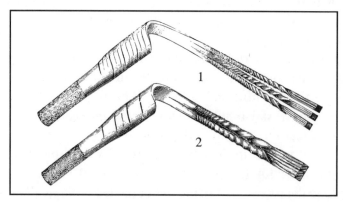

Process of barrel welding: 1. Three-iron Damascus 2. Two-iron Damascus*

mandrel in a spiral and forge welding the resulting circumferential seam. The hoop stress was now borne mostly by the strips in tension, instead of along the longitudinal seam. This approach became the fundamental concept of Damascus barrels (*see W. W. Greener, 1893*).

The process was soon perfected. High-quality thin strips were made by rolling, drawing, hammering, and twisting layers of best available [low-carbon] steel and best available [low-carbon] malleable iron when hot – thereby condensing and aligning the grain in the most advantageous direction. Nonmetallic impurities were also broken up and dispersed. Approximately 18 pounds of very high-quality gunmaking iron and steel were required to produce a normal 3½-pound set of finished barrels.

This system produced excellent results from the late 1700s forward, and contrary to popular beliefs, could serve equally as well today were it not for the amount and quality of labor involved. Costs were always high. They would be prohibitive today.

English barrel makers perfected Damascus of higher quality than similar products of Belgium and Spain. One characteristic, greater hardness, was critical to meet requirements of choke boring, which by 1875 was rapidly becoming accepted, in parallel with the now well-established breechloaders.

It was during this period of shotgun development that Sir Joseph Whitworth perfected his fluid pressed steel, which limited the size of flaws in steel ingots. A uniform steel product was now available to barrel makers that was harder than Damascus, could match the strength of Damascus, and was well suited to choke boring. About the same time, machining tools were developed that could bore long straight holes, thereby making it practical to produce tubes from solid forgings.

Steel barrels were now possible. They were thin enough and strong enough to compare in weight with Damascus, but they were harder, an advantage that made it possible for the choke section to be thinner. This steel product, coupled with new manufacturing procedures, brought to barrel making art the additional feature of lumps forged integrally with the barrels (*see Figure 2*). Moreover, finished barrels would withstand more banging abuse by careless owners or loaders, a valuable characteristic.

Two alternatives were now available: Damascus and high-quality steel. Which was better? The controversy over this issue has survived for 120 years to the present day. There are exponents of both perspectives: the elegant beauty of Damascus versus the more practical steel equivalent. The fact that steel barrels were less expensive drove new Damascus barrels from the market about seventy years ago and gave rise to the erroneous conclusion that steel is also a vastly superior product, which is not the case.

In 1888, the Birmingham Proof House made an exhaustive test comparison of steel and Damascus barrels, which proved conclusively that there was no technical superiority to be found between best English Damascus and best English gun-barrel steel. Today, either type of barrel, with current nitro proofing, can be considered equally usable. Beauty and levels of care are another matter.

The strangely consistent, but totally unjustified, bad reputation that Damascus barrels have in America probably comes from low-quality material used in inexpensive trade guns, which found their way into foreign markets from various manufacturers. A related issue that also may have contributed to the formation of negative popular opinion involves the issue of gunpowder.

A Primer on Powder

Misconceptions surround the development of gunpowder from the original black powder to modern nitro powders. Failure to understand certain fundamentals of powder evolution has no doubt contributed to distrust of Damascus barrels in America, where it is almost universally, but erroneously, assumed that these barrels cannot withstand the modern pressures (a meaningless term) of nitro powder.

It was not until 1862 that a viable alternative to black powder appeared on the market. This first successful smokeless nitro powder, by Schultze, was followed by EC powder in 1882. Both of these powders, and many others manufactured before World War I, were bulk powders. This means that they shared an equivalency. Any weight (or volumetric) charge of one was equal to an identical weight (or volumetric) charge of another, and to the same charge of black powder.

This consistency was purposely maintained, so loading equipment then in use could accommodate black powder or any of the new smokeless nitro powders without any inherent dangers.

An illustration from Greener's 1893 work clearly shows that the bulk (volume) of the early nitro powders was meant to correspond to the same bulk (volume) of black powder, which made it possible to use existing loading tools and shotguns:

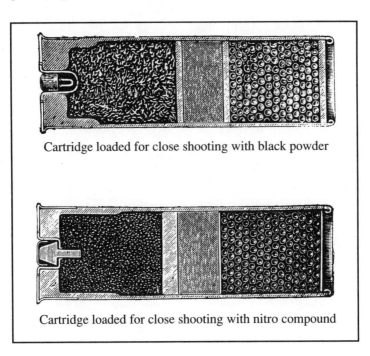

Cartridge loaded for close shooting with black powder

Cartridge loaded for close shooting with nitro compound

Bulk powder substitutes that supplanted black powder had the advantage of being smokeless and much cleaner, but were obviously intended for guns then in general use, most of which had Damascus barrels. So far so good! A dram is a dram is a dram.

In 1888, however, Alfred Nobel introduced a radically different smokeless powder that was dense, meaning it took a much smaller amount to duplicate the performance of black and bulk smokeless powders. Now the issue of suitable loads became quite critical, and predictable problems arose.

To enjoy the benefits of smokeless powder, shooters had to be very cautious to determine whether bulk powder or new dense smokeless powder was being used in the loading of cartridges. In the event the volumetric powder charge was not properly reduced for a dense powder, failures occurred. After an unhappy transition period, dram equivalent ratings became widely used and reduced the danger. It is fundamental to recognize, however, that barrel pressures for black, bulk, or modern (dense) smokeless powders, for a reasonable muzzle velocity and an identical shot charge, are in the same range and always have been. In other words, there is no such thing as modern pressures for nitro powders.

European versus American Approaches

Europeans seem to have had few problems with the concept of dense nitro powders and how to use them. In 1904, the British introduced nitro proof to provide a secure basis for the increasing use of new dense powder. In 1925, the use of nitro proof became compulsory in Britain. It is noteworthy, however, that English Damascus barrels continued to be favored by many shooters. Only after World War I, when inexpensive steel suitable for barrels greatly reduced the price of guns, did steel barrels finally supplant English Damascus barrels for best guns. During the period of transition, Damascus barrels were still offered, but at a substantial increase in cost.

In America, the situation was quite different. Most early shotguns produced in America used Belgium Damascus. Imported trade guns used even poorer quality barrels. Later, after the introduction of dense nitro powders, there was a distinct trend to escalate loadings of both powder and shot. This American preference for heavier loads, coupled with a total absence of proof laws, soon resulted in failures of lower quality Damascus barrels.

The problem was approached and a solution achieved by redesigning the barrel thickness profile and by using new inexpensive barrel steels. Naturally, thicker barrels meant greater overall gun weight, a feature that has characterized American guns even into the modern era. Ironically, the post World War II trend toward shorter barrels for machine made guns can probably be attributed to the desire of some shooters to decrease total weight. This solution, however, carries with it some unfortunate features of balance and performance. Barrel length is discussed in some detail in Chapter 10.

Evolution of Sleeving

While it is well established that fine Damascus barrels are equivalent to best quality steel barrels, the same composition of materials used for the tubes is too soft for the barrel lumps. To achieve proper results, barrel makers filed up hard steel to produce the lumps, which were then dovetailed and brazed into place on Damascus barrels. This procedure had the advantage of lumps with good wearing qualities, but the corollary disadvantage of occasional separation that required rebrazing.

After the advent of Sir Joseph Whitworth's fluid pressed steel and later metallurgical developments, lumps could be forged with the barrel blank, one-half to each tube. Chopper lump barrels, named because of their resemblance to a common chopping tool, came into being. This integral forging had the obvious advantage of eliminating separation problems, but it resulted in a material for the lumps that was softer than desirable since the barrels and the lumps were of the same composition.

Around 1900, Birmingham barrel makers, always alert to less expensive techniques of production, introduced a third basic approach that would permit greater use of machine tools and avoid much of the costly hand labor in filing. Because chopper lump barrels were long and clumsy, they did not lend themselves well to machining, so Birmingham makers concluded that the two components should be produced separately and joined, but not in the same manner as Damascus barrels.

New lumps were machined from a piece of hard steel about three inches in length, configured to consist of the breech end of the barrels as well as the traditional lumps. Two large holes were then bored into this monoblock, which permitted insertion and soldering of two round barrel tubes. This clever process achieved desirable hardness in the lumps, securely joined barrel tubes to the monoblock, and was less expensive. It was, however, an approach shunned by the London gun trade as not suitable for best guns, so it was used only in Birmingham on less expensive guns. After World War I, Italian gunmakers, notably Beretta, began successfully to make double-barrel guns in this fashion.

In the 1950s skilled gunmaking craftsmen were becoming increasingly rare in England, which reduced the availability of best quality new guns. The price of fine double-barrel guns steadily climbed. Disparity between supply and demand was somewhat mitigated, however, by the substantial number of old, very serviceable English guns existing throughout Britain and in other locations worldwide.

Unfortunately, barrels on many of these old guns had been ruined, by corrosive primers, by abuse, or sometimes by misuse. Since the cost of rebarreling and fitting new barrels to the old action was prohibitive for all save the very finest guns, a salvaging innovation was developed by English gunmakers makers. First, ribs were removed from the old barrels. Then the old barrels were sawed off about three inches from the breech, still in a thickened section. Using the Birmingham approach, old chambers were bored out to produce a monoblock. The final steps consisted of fastening in new barrel tubes and attaching the old ribs.

This sleeving system saved a great number of wonderful guns from the scrap heap and put them in the hands of many people who appreciated fine guns but could not afford new guns or costly new barrels. All in all, this was a satisfying alternative.

Chamber Sleeving – a Recent Innovation

A more recent sleeving development makes it possible to convert quality 10-bore and 16-bore double guns to more popular 12-bore and 20-bore gauges, respectively, thereby saving these guns from oblivion. Interestingly, it was a cartridge modification that paved the way for these sleeving conversions.

During the 1970s, one-piece plastic wads were introduced and perfected. They replaced time-honored, but less effective, felt over-powder wads. One of several advantages of plastic wads is the expansion characteristic of the cup-shaped base, which tends to fill an oversized bore.

This conclusion is verified by published research and unpublished experiments by internal ballistics experts. Performance of oversized bores (and lengthened forcing cones) is significantly improved by virtue of the expansion capabilities of one-piece plastic wads, a performance that is not achievable with felt wads.

Several gun dealers in America found that chambers of 10-bore and 16-bore double guns could be bored out and then lined with thin sleeves. This process converted them, in effect, to overbored 12-bore and 20-bore guns without forcing cones. The resulting performance is very good from the standpoint of patterns.

In addition, these converted 12-bore and 20-bore guns are heavier and more nearly fit the American ideal of suitable weight, as opposed to English preference for lighter field guns. Once again, a sleeving application came to the rescue of quality guns (with unpopular gauges) and gave them a new useful life.

Barrel Filing and Finishing

The finished surface of a London best barrel is incredibly smooth. Even to the unpracticed eye, this perfectly even surface, as well as the characteristic of a profiled curvature, can easily be seen by sighting down the outside of the barrel. Each one is finished entirely by hand.

Tubes and ribs are first struck-up along the length of the barrel by using striking irons. Striking is followed by smoothing and polishing with finer and finer emery cloth until the proper standard is attained, which is a surface smoothed to a tolerance of less than 0.0005 inch. This tedious process takes up to one week of work on a pair of barrels.

Barrels of lesser guns have a finished surface that is normally wavy and slightly wrinkled, even if it is well polished. Machine finished barrels are neither smooth nor polished. This particular distinction of best guns is readily apparent even to those not technically competent to judge other, less obvious merits.

Blacking and Browning

A widely used term for finish on mass-produced gun barrels is called bluing. These barrels are dipped in a liquid chemical bath that colors the steel, usually with a bluish cast, and produces a wavy and somewhat uneven finish. Wearing qualities are generally not of a high standard with this process.

British gun barrels, with the exception of Damascus, have an even black finish attained by an entirely different, time-consuming process. Completed barrels, in the white, are cleaned and coated with a special mixture. Then they are allowed to rust under controlled conditions, after which they are cleaned and resubmitted to the rusting process, over and over again. When the surface reaches precisely the right color, oil is applied to halt the process. This rust blacking takes about two weeks of expert attention, but produces a deep, even, long-wearing color.

This same general process was, and is, still used for Damascus barrels, but the process continues for about one month. The composite iron and steel layers of Damascus require a different secret mixture and react to the rusting and cleaning process in a distinct fashion, so that beautiful patterning shows through at the end. It produces brown and silver highlights (*see Figures 11, 12, and 23*). Damascus barrels are therefore said to be browned. It is possible, however, to blacken Damascus barrels to make them nearly indistinguishable from steel barrels.

✤ Chapter 3 ✤

Locks and Actions

No part of a gun varies more than its locks.

– Sir Ralph Payne-Gallwey

Overview

Just as some experts consider barrels the most important part of a gun, others are of the opinion that the locks and action are the *sine qua non* of the breechloading shotgun. Arguments supporting this position have great merit. It is the complex combination of action and locks that provides a rigid connection between the stock and the barrels, and permits easy loading of cartridges, enables the gun to be fired safely, and makes consistent trigger pulls possible. Without these features, use of the shotgun for hitting moving targets is hard to imagine.

Surprisingly, the modern hammerless gun is really little changed in many respects from muzzleloading flintlocks of the late 1700s. From a functional standpoint, pulling the trigger on either type of gun moves a sear that allows a tumbler (hammer) to fall and fire the powder. Nothing is very different, at least in principle. Modern hammerless guns contain the moving parts inside the action, while flintlocks divide moving components almost equally between the inside and outside of the external plate.

More fundamental are the different requirements introduced by breechloading. Before this massive step could be accomplished, problems associated with a gun that breaks open had to be solved. Solutions abounded.

In this presentation it is impractical to treat, even superficially, all the ingenious systems that appeared during the last half of the 1800s. The intention here is to present an overview of certain basic types of locks, actions, and operating mechanisms, primarily those that were most successful and are still in use today. At the conclusion of Part I, a selected bibliography is included. For the technically inclined, a review of this literature will reveal details of many remarkable designs that led eventually to systems that survived. It is literally a story of mechanical evolution.

Definitions

Any discussion of locks and actions faces the inherent danger of making general statements about their mechanical systems. In the relationships between locks and actions, nearly every possible combination or adaptation has been tried at one time or another. Inevitably, exceptions can be made about any general conclusion. The effort here will be to summarize the basic information in a straightforward manner.

As a starting point, what constitutes an action and a lock are their functions. The action joins the stock to the barrels in a manner that permits breaking the gun open for loading. Locks perform the mechanical transmission of the trigger pull to the firing of the cartridge.

Physically, the action is essentially a housing of one type or another that incorporates the hinge (or cross) pin, a device to bolt the barrels closed, and the opening/closing mechanisms. The action also holds or contains the locks, usually. Locks consist of an integral arrangement of sear, springs, and tumbler (hammer). These definitions are simplified, for interrelationships make it difficult to separate these components.

In our discussion of locks, basic types of successful locks will be treated separately from a discussion of types of operating mechanisms that enable opening, closing, and bolting of the breechloading gun, as well as cocking of the locks. It should be kept in mind that a structural action had to house and/or accommodate all of these elements, regardless of various combinations employed on any particular gun.

Locks

Three main types of locks have survived the process of breechloader evolution: sidelocks, boxlocks, and various types of trigger plate mechanisms. All of the guns pictured in Part I are sidelocks except for Figure 12, which is a trigger plate mechanism and Figures 38 and 41 (lower gun), which are boxlocks.

Sidelocks: The sidelock, by virtue of its lengthy configuration, and consequent relation to the trigger, is well-balanced mechanically, which is a paramount advantage. The layout of the sidelock also permits the bar of the action (which fits to the flats of the barrels) to be relatively solid. This inherent strength, in turn, enables the entire action to be smaller. The head of the stock can then be firmly bedded to the solid back of a relatively thin and shapely action body. The finished product of action and stock is very graceful in appearance in addition to its mechanical excellence.

The disadvantages of the sidelock, from technical and cost standpoints, are the large number of individual parts and attendant complexities of production. High quality materials and highly skilled craftsmen are required to construct and regulate sidelocks.

Boxlocks: The boxlock was developed to produce a less expensive system than the complex sidelock. The design objective of greater simplicity was accomplished with the boxlock; however, in most instances boxlock guns are bulkier than sidelocks, resulting in a partial sacrifice of graceful appearance. The advantage of few parts, plus the ease of production by machine tools, did succeed in reducing production costs. Boxlocks were never popular with London makers. As a consequence, they are generally not regarded as best guns by the trade.

The boxlock's less desirable qualities stem from inherent limitations of mechanical layout. Trigger pulls are sometimes erratic and hard to adjust because of the positioning and unequal length of the lever arms of the sears. It is also difficult to fit a safety mechanism (intercepting sear) that prevents accidental firing from impact, such as in a case when a gun is accidentally dropped. Because of shorter overall length and ensuing fit requirements, the body of the action is basically hollow, which requires it to be deeper and wider to achieve strength. This bulkier framework transmits to the stock, which must also be thicker, all of which detracts from the high standard of beauty and weight distribution afforded by sidelocks.

Trigger Plate Mechanisms: This interesting family of mechanisms developed early in the breechloading era. Many of the various trigger plate designs were marvels of complexity, and yet they enabled the gunmaker to produce a stylish and elegant gun. Although these mechanisms were abandoned for the most part as too difficult and costly to make, the original concept still survives with some Scottish gunmakers.

Much more significant is an adaptation of the trigger plate mechanism used on the majority of over/under double-barrel guns manufactured worldwide. One Italian gunmaker has developed a successful refinement that makes it possible for the locks to be removed as a unit for cleaning and repair. Now Holland & Holland has adopted this Italian removable trigger plate type design innovation to offer a London produced over/under gun that incorporates this system in basic principle.

On the other hand, these types of over/under guns, though less expensive, do not compare well in grace, form, and liveliness with London-style sidelock over/under guns, which will be discussed in more detail later in this chapter.

Operating Mechanisms (*see Figures 3 through 8*)

Development of the breechloader involved experimentation with an amazing variety of operating mechanisms to enable opening, closing, and bolting of the action and cocking of the locks. Most of these arrangements did not survive into the 1900s because of their inconvenience, high production costs, or a dawning awareness that massive strength was not required to keep a gun closed when firing normal loads.

Authorities agree that the most significant advance came with the invention of the Purdey sliding bolt of 1863, often called the Purdey bolt. Without a question, it became the dominant type of bolt for locking the barrels to the action of double-barrel guns and rifles. With few exceptions, all ultimately successful operating mechanisms have used the Purdey sliding bolt to engage and disengage matching cuts or bites on the lumps (*see Figure 2*).

Various supplemental locking devices (third fasteners) were used in conjunction with the Purdey bolt, such as cross bolts and rising bites. The Purdey bolt, however, combined with double underlocking lugs, is now accepted as a basic requirement to prevent the breech from opening when the gun is fired under normal circumstances (*see Figures 13 through 16*).

Of the many opening and closing operating mechanisms, five types are considered to be the most successful: rotary (Jones) underlever, thumbhole, snap underlever, sidelever, and top lever.

Rotary (Jones) Underlever (*Figure 3*): Of the five types, only the rotary underlever does not incorporate the Purdey bolt, which it preceded. This truly great system of bolting barrels to action was patented by Henry Jones in 1859. When the patent lapsed in 1862, supposedly for want of a £50 stamp, it was adopted by almost every gunmaker. Jones lived to be over one hundred years of age, and it is said that he never in his lifetime compiled this sum in pounds sterling.

The rotary underlever is referred to as an *inert* system, because it will not lock by itself. It requires part of the rotary movement of the underlever to be assisted manually. It is, however, tremendously strong and has been used successfully on everything from 20-bore game guns to 4-bore rifles well into this century. Lang even adapted the Jones rotary bolt to work with a top lever in his hammer guns, which resulted in a very strong and convenient snap action.

Thumbhole (*Figure 4*): The thumbhole mechanism was the first opening device to be used in concert with the Purdey bolt. It not only functions well, but provides equal convenience of access to both right-handed or left-handed shooters. The thumbhole lever is attached to the bottom of the Purdey bolt and has a rather short lever arm.

Snap Underlever (*Figures 5 and 6*): This opening mechanism more or less replaced the thumbhole by bringing the connecting arm back over the trigger guard and greatly increasing leverage. The thumb pad can hang below the rear of the trigger guard, as favored by Woodward, or can be bent 90 degrees to the right or left. The snap underlever therefore works equally well for both right-handed and left-handed shooters.

Sidelever (*Figure 7*): Arguably, the most graceful and effective opening mechanism is the sidelever. It was often employed by Grant and Boss. Every London best maker used the sidelever at one time or another. Grant still makes them today as an option for side-by-side shotguns. The connecting arm of the sidelever attaches to the bottom of the Purdey bolt and can be easily adapted to the right or left side of the action.

Top Lever (*Figure 8*): The Scott spindle of 1865 was a major conceptual advance that has subsequently become known as the top lever. It has, for all practical purposes, become the standard opening mechanism for almost all modern shotguns and double rifles. It is small, reasonably inexpensive to make as compared with other types of openers, and works well. The only disadvantages are the short lever arm and the fact that it attaches to the rear of the Purdey bolt.

This latter disadvantage requires modification or rearrangement of some of the vital elements in the gun's mechanism, the most notable being the tumblers (hammers) and strikers (firing pins) of over/under guns. Because of several design aspects, it is also difficult to make a left-handed top lever. It is nonetheless irrefutable that the combination of the Purdey bolt and the Scott spindle is a grand union.

Over/Under Guns

Over/under guns present action and operating mechanism design problems that are not easy to overcome. These technical problems include eccentric strikers (firing pins), deep actions, and heavy total weights. Even more complexities are encountered when over/unders are built as sidelocks, in an effort to make them more graceful and effective.

In the early 1900s, Boss and Woodward solved the depth problem with bifurcated bites on the rear of the barrels, and trunions in place of a hinge pin. They were thus able to produce a sidelock over/under that can be very graceful, well balanced, and reasonably light (*see Figures 28 and 42*). Even today, several London gunmakers will produce these best quality sidelock over/unders of classic design. They are, however, difficult to make and correspondingly expensive to own.

After World War II, Beretta adapted this design to a mass-produced gun in both sidelock and trigger plate type mechanisms. These guns are relatively inexpensive and widely sold. Other Italian makers have copied and altered the London sidelock design and have produced some largely machine made, yet serviceable guns of quality, although not London best.

✤ Chapter 4 ✤

Stocks

There is no definite authority for the prevailing fashion in gunstocks, and the dimensions and shape of this part of the gun have given rise to more frequent discussion amongst gunmakers and sportsmen than anything else connected with shooting.

– W. W. Greener

The Stock and Its Development

The third basic component of the modern shotgun is the stock. Although barrel advocates are steadfast in believing that nothing compares in importance with the telltale tubes, and action/lock fanciers are convinced that the guts of the gun constitute its technical essence, a fine shot, given his say, will often maintain it is the stock that reigns supreme. From the standpoint of a rationale based on function, this position is not only defensible, but reasonable. A properly shaped and well-balanced stock undeniably has a dramatic impact on the ability of the shooter, whether amateur or accomplished, to hit a moving target with regularity.

To this functional argument, however, must be added the equally compelling importance of aesthetics. The beauty of wood figuring in the buttstock of a gun immediately draws the eye of the beholder. The size of the stock itself, coupled with its rich coloration, constitutes such an obvious attraction that other components of the gun are virtually overshadowed. To the natural beauty of endless variations in wood characteristics is added the skill of the stock finisher, who can highlight the strengths of any pattern with proper staining and/or coloring.

Wherever these debates about the preeminence of lock, stock, or barrel may lead, those who incline toward the stock can always rest their case on history. Until the French began to make stocks around 1750 that approach current shape and dimensions, wing shooting had been somewhat of an ineffective novelty, even though it was attempted as early as the first part of the seventeenth century. Game was usually shot on the ground or on water, preferably in concentrations or groups.

The gunstock, as it is known today, was essentially perfected just before 1800 by Joseph Manton, acknowledged by many as "the greatest artist in firearms that the world ever produced." His beautifully crafted stocks set a pattern that has changed little in its basic form. While it is true that the action of the breechloading shotgun now interrupts the continuous flow of stock that characterized muzzleloaders, both guns have the same feel when handled and when mounted. The one-piece stock has been replaced by a butt and a fore-end, but the depth and width of the butt and the shape of the comb and belly are remarkably similar. It may therefore be said that the stock of a late model (mid-1800s) best London fowling piece is really very little different from a current best London shotgun (*see Figure 1*).

Modern shotgun stocks function to align the individual shooter's master eye with the barrels and to steady the gun through the swing, including firing recoil. Details of stock configuration have been perfected over a period of 150 years of development through trial and error (about 1750 to 1900). The fine-tuning process was led by English gunmakers and was driven by demanding requirements of their clientele, who shot game in great numbers and who competed actively in popular live pigeon matches.

It was the practice of some of the better London gunmakers to attend competitive pigeon (trap) matches to assist their clients and to observe the experimental changes they were constantly testing. The first meeting of the committee that wrote the Hurlingham Club Rules (basically the FITASC rules of today) was held at Stephen Grant's St. James Street store on 23 February 1869. Until pigeon shooting from traps was abolished at Hurlingham in December of 1905, Boss, Grant, Purdey, or their representatives were present at most of the major matches. On-site observation of gun performance under demanding shooting conditions obviously provided valuable feedback.

Knowledgeable shooters brought a wealth of practical experience to the gunmaker's table. They also had the money to have their ideas about stocking, balance, and weight incorporated into the making of exceptional guns. London gunmakers, in fierce competition to serve prominent buyers, freely offered technical advice. They were, however, willing to make the types of stocks these shooters wanted, even if it meant a departure from traditional forms. Eventually, the more successful experiments with dimensions and shapes evolved into a product that spread throughout the gun trade and became available to everyone. Modern stock dimensions, and related issues, are presented in Chapter 19.

Wood for Gunstocks

Almost every type of wood has been tried at one time or another for gunstocks. Vast experimentation has revealed that some woods are more beautiful, some are more workable and others are more durable. Ultimately, however, there is no contest. French walnut offers the ideal combination of beauty, weight, stability, workability, and durability. It is the preferred choice for high-quality guns.

Because of the increasing scarcity of this particular variety of walnut, the price is correspondingly high, which means that guns of lesser quality must resort to walnuts with less favorable characteristics. The scientific name for all walnuts is *Juglaus regia,* but woodworking qualities and other properties vary considerably, apparently the result of climatic and soil chemistry differences.

Weight

Because the dimensions of a buttstock are basically fixed (within guideline limits), the density of the wood greatly affects the overall weight and balance. Very dense wood, such as a Circassian (Turkish) walnut, must be hollowed out to reduce weight.

By contrast, a very light wood requires weight, usually lead, to be placed into the butt, which causes a strange weight distribution and a clumsy feel to the entire gun. The weight adaptations required for French walnut are minimal.

Stability

After a tree has been harvested, choice parts must be properly cut into stock blanks with great care. Then a process of several years of air drying begins until moisture content of the wood stabilizes, which ensures that there will be no shrinking or cracking when blanks are worked into shape.

Good blanks have always been valuable and sought after, as evidenced by the number that have undergone the drying process.

Today, demand greatly exceeds the steadily shrinking supply, which has had a significant impact on price. A respectable French walnut blank has become quite expensive.

Fortunately, once the blank is fitted to the action, shaped, and finished, it lasts for an indefinite period under conditions of reasonable care. Stocks well over a century old are still ruggedly serviceable, with only a few surface cracks around the tang or locks to betray their age. Indications are that these veterans may carry on in service for yet another century or more.

Workability

Workability is the characteristic that defines how stocker and finisher can use their tools and techniques on wood. If the wood is too brittle, tools of the stocker tend to chip and split the wood. The result is an uneven surface. When the finisher attempts to checker such wood, the diamonds are prone to chip off and ruin the appearance of the work. It is critical that points of the checkering be sharp to prevent the hand from slipping as the gun recoils.

Conversely, wood that is too soft will not hold its inletting, will compress with time, and cause the stock to loosen from the action. Points of the checkering will wear and become smooth. It has long been said, in tribute, that French walnut cuts like butter and wears like iron (*see Figure 25*).

Durability

In the normal course of its life, the stock must resist impact from various knocks on the gun. With most good wood, dents can be lifted by steaming. Of greater significance is the durability required where the head of the stock joins the action of the gun. It is at this narrowed point that the entire force of recoil focuses on the end grain of the stock and is then transmitted to trigger hand and shoulder of the shooter. Not only is the quality of the wood called into play, but the stocker must do a near perfect job of mating metal to wood at this point to avoid stress concentrations (*see Figures 26a and 26b*). If the load is not evenly distributed, compression will cause the stock to become loose on the action.

Checkering

There is a common misconception that checkering is simply a handsome decoration. A significant part of firing recoil is absorbed by the right hand, which requires a crisp, nonslip surface to grip. Quality checkering on quality walnut permits the shooter to hold the gun firmly, while absorbing recoil and controlling the gun for a second shot. Very fine (close line) checkering or flat point checkering fails to accomplish this intended purpose.

Stock Finish

Naturally, the last step in producing a gunstock is the finish. There is perhaps no better example of the difference between a best gun and a mass-produced shotgun than stock finishing. The process begins with a stock that is already basically configured to the desired individual dimensions. Final smoothness and precise shape are attained by hand, using successively finer abrasives, templates, and an expert eye. The end product of a perfectly contoured, smooth surface can be appreciated by anyone who loves the feel and shape of wood that is worked by a master craftsman.

The finisher then applies staining and sealing ingredients, followed by his own secret oil. A final oil finish is accomplished by successive thin applications that are each hand rubbed and allowed to dry. The process of adding layer after rubbed layer, at almost daily intervals, takes about two to six weeks.

Such a finish not only has restrained elegance but is also extremely practical. Inevitable wear marks that come with usage can easily be repaired by rubbing on a single drop of boiled linseed oil and allowing it to dry, a luxury not possible with the lacquered finishes of production guns.

Care

Even with the highest quality of French walnut, the owner must take care to maintain the innate excellence of the gunstock. Perhaps the greatest danger, aside from outright abuse and breakage, is exposure to gun oil entering the head of the stock through the action. This inadvertent entry will, over time, soften the wood at a critical point and cause the stock to loosen.

A prudent owner will not allow gun oil to enter around the triggers, striker (firing pin) holes, safety, or top lever. He is also well advised to store the gun with barrels down so that any excess oil will drain away from the head of the stock. These precautions will preserve the life of the gunstock.

✤ Chapter 5 ✤

Choke

Choke lengthens your reach, but may lighten your bag.

– Old Hampshire saying

Historical Background

It is a curious anomaly in the long history of shotgun development that the exact origin of choke is not well established in spite of its relatively recent appearance on the scene after 1865. A cloud of uncertainty seems to veil popular anecdotes and makes it difficult to credit a single source of inspiration.

American gun folklore lays claim to choke as having been first conceived and perfected shortly after the Civil War by an Illinois market hunter by the name of Fred Kimble. Actual records of scores in live pigeon matches verify that Mr. Kimble handled his muzzleloading shotgun quite well. Credibility is eroded, however, by some of the apocryphal claims regarding the performance of his choke-bored guns. There is considerable doubt that a muzzleloading shotgun with heavily choked barrels could be loaded with the hard overpowder wads then in use. Unfortunately, none of these barrels with heavy chokes seems to have survived.

There are, however, some rather vague written descriptions of the way English barrel makers produced choke in muzzleloaders. These accounts would suggest that early efforts were a form of recessed choke, still used occasionally today on barrels that have been cut off. The effectiveness of such a procedure has always been marginal. It is therefore unlikely that a recessed type choke could produce the lofty results claimed by early choke enthusiasts.

William Rochester Pape, in his English patent of 1866, described how a shotgun barrel was to be choke bored, almost as an aside to the main thrust of his patent, which dealt with a bolting system. Mr. Pape certainly did little to protect his patent, or to capitalize on choke as an invention, for he failed to pay the £100 renewal fee due in 1873. His patent protection thereby lapsed. There is, moreover, credible evidence that many other barrel borers were incorporating some type of choke boring for breechloading guns during this same period.

It is interesting, for example, to reflect on records of the pattern trials of 1866, sponsored by *Field* magazine. The two top-ranked guns, based on performance, were choke bored. Of further interest is the limited amount of choke reported, which by today's standards only reflect an improved cylinder.

Roper's patent of 1867 is remarkable as a harbinger of things to come. The secondary invention of this patent was a screw-on choke tube, which never seemed to gain acceptance. About a hundred years later, Jess Briley of Texas perfected a way to install a removable screw-in choke tube without spoiling the external appearance of the barrels. It has rightfully attained broad usage and will be discussed later in this chapter.

Although W. W. Greener did not invent choke boring, he soon became its foremost champion among contemporary gunmakers. He was always ready to capitalize on this advocacy as evidenced by his self-serving book, *Choke-Bore Guns*, which was published in 1876. To his credit, Greener recommended in this book the lengthening of the chamber forcing cones to improve patterns. Some 110 years later, mainstream shotgun manufacturers have adopted the incremental advantage to be gained by this method.

By the 1870s, breechloading guns were winning most live pigeon matches and gun pattern trials because the bores were choked. About this time, development of a chilled (alloyed) shot of greater hardness than pure lead also played a significant role in performance.

An Overview of Choke

Best guns were developed and produced not by science, but as an art. Nowhere is the truth of this more evident than in barrel choking. In spite of many attempts at a scientific approach, and endless testing of theory versus pattern results, choke largely remains a matter that defies precise technical definition.

The simplistic definition of choke as constriction at the muzzle of the barrel, normally expressed in thousandths of an inch differences from the diameter of the bore, is deceptive, if not misleading. It is nonetheless the only convenient starting point to compare and describe choke.

Beyond the actual amount of constriction in choke is the fascinating means by which it is achieved, or the shape of the choke. Here lies artistry and departure from scientific design. Logic would suggest that narrow guideline limits have evolved to define a basic shape and length, which is only partially true. Chokes vary in length. They are seldom greater than 3 inches or less than an astonishing minimum of about ³/₈ inch.

Certain general observations regarding shape can, however, be drawn. Chokes almost always are divided into two sections that characterize individual configuration. Constriction is accomplished by the taper or lead, which is normally followed by the parallel or flat.

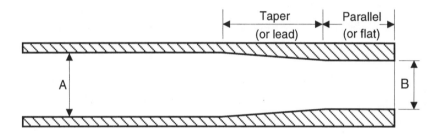

A : Bore
A minus B : Constriction

Nearly every barrel maker has his favorite shape. Variations are the norm, not the exception. Personal beliefs of the choke man have become rooted in tradition. There is insufficient compelling scientific evidence to warrant a departure from this practice of individual preference.

Patterns and Choke

Entire books and many technical papers have been written about patterns that result from various types and constrictions of choke. These disquisitions, while interesting to the technically inclined, are more than average shooters want to know. His primary concern lies in the answers to certain basic questions of field performance. The attempt here will be to present only those summary conclusions that highlight the issues involved. A selected bibliography is found at the conclusion of Part I for those who wish to pursue the matter further.

The following table for a 12-bore gun is instructive:

Constriction	Percentage of Shot in Pattern	Percentage Gain
(In thousandths/inch)	**(In 30-inch circle @ 40 yd.)**	
0.000	40%	–
0.010	55%	15%
0.020	65%	10%
0.030	70%	5%
0.040	75%	5%

These data cover the entire range from no choke, or cylinder bore, to what is generally accepted as maximum effective constriction from the bore diameter, 0.040-inch. It is immediately apparent that equal steps of constriction do not produce like improvements in the so-called killing pattern (30-inch diameter circle) at 40 yards. Initial increments produce substantial results. Final tightening of the choke is far less rewarding in terms of a percentage increase in pellet count and therefore in range extension.

From a practical standpoint, 12-bore constrictions over 0.035-inch are not generally considered to be effective, because shot distribution becomes too center dense, not to mention the added skill requirements imposed on the shooter.

At the other end of the spectrum, patterns of a cylinder bore (no choke) have a poor distribution of pellets, as well as a low percentage of total pellets in the standard 30-inch circle at 40 yards. Even a very slight constriction, say 0.002-inch, greatly improves distribution and produces quite acceptable patterns, though it only slightly increases the pellet count.

As further illustration of the surprising world of choke phenomena, consider the following rather unrelated observations:

1. If the diameter of the choke remains fixed (i.e., the flat), and if bore is slightly enlarged, the resulting pattern will

be tighter, because the net effect has been to increase constriction. Should this process, however, exceed the accepted limit of constriction for any particular gauge of gun, the overchoking will actually reduce the pattern pellet count and adversely affect the distribution.

2. The size of the shot to be used affects the optimum lengthof the lead, or taper. Larger shot will pattern better with more length, i.e., a less abrupt slope. Larger shot also seems to require a longer flat or parallel.

3. Steel (iron) shot apparently requires about one-half the constriction of lead shot to obtain the same percentage pattern.

4. The length of the barrel, within normal limits, has no significant effect on the performance of choke.

Cartridges and Choke

Today's English gunmakers are inclined to use a mathematical approach to the amount of constriction, and a choke shape that reflects a preference based on their individual experience. The following table is the standard Barrel Choke Chart of one London best maker:

ATKIN GRANT & LANG
BARREL CHOKE CHART

Bore	Bore Dia.	Imp. Cyl.	$1/4$	$1/2$	$3/4$	Full
12	0.729	0.001-5	0.006-14	0.015-22	0.023-30	0.031-35
20	0.615	0.001-3	0.004-11	0.012-18	0.019-26	0.027-30
28	0.550	0.001-3	0.004-9	0.010-15	0.016-20	0.021-24
410	0.410	0.001-2	0.003-6	0.007-11	0.012-15	0.016-18
% Pellets in 30-in. Circle at 40 yds.	40-50		50-60	60-65	65-70	70-75

It is important to realize that the measurement of choke constriction is only an indication of what pattern percentages the shooter will actually achieve. This apparent inconsistency derives from the almost endless variety of cartridges presently in use, and the shape of the choke itself.

In the past, a London maker would indicate inside the gun case the percentage performance of each barrel choke, which matched the buyer's specified desires. His certainty in doing so was based on the practice of also supplying cartridges, thereby ensuring that he could control the type of wad, powder, and shot to be used in the gun.

Cartridge components available today alter the picture completely. For a given barrel of, for instance, one-half (modified) choke, any pattern percentage from 50 to 70 percent can be obtained by varying the material and hardness of the overpowder wad, burning speed and amount of the powder, hardness and roundness of the shot pellets, and use or absence of a shot sleeve. Generally speaking, a heavy charge of fast-burning powder behind a hard felt wad with a load of soft, irregular shot and no shot sleeve will produce a large spread, i.e., a low percentage pattern.

Conversely, a light charge of slow-burning powder behind a one-piece plastic wad (with a well-designed collapsing column and thick shot sleeve) and medium-size shot that is hard (6 percent antimony), round, well-graded, and nickel-plated will produce a dense, well-distributed, high-percentage pattern from the same one-half choke.

In view of this variation of pattern results driven solely by the type of cartridge, the following conclusion is not outrageous: A shooter could own but one gun with identical one-half chokes in each barrel and use this gun effectively on every game target from pen-raised quail to the most daunting of high-driven pheasants by varying the types of cartridges. He would, however, be faced with a cartridge selection incubus of staggering proportions. A more reasonable solution rests with consistent use of cartridges with good components and moderate loads, coupled with a gun, or guns, intelligently choked for the intended purpose.

Temperature and Altitude Considerations

Pattern performance of cartridges and chokes is also affected by temperature and altitude. Although temperature effect is relatively minor, colder ambient temperatures do slow slightly the burn rate of the powder and increase the density of the air, which tends to slow the shot and open the pattern.

The effect of altitude is much more noticeable. For each increase of a thousand feet in altitude, the standard pattern (30-inch circle at 40 yards) will pick up two to three percent more pellets. Consider shooting box pigeons at the club in Pachuca, Hidalgo, Mexico, where the rings are at an elevation of 7,800 feet, as compared to a performance at sea level. A given barrel, choke, and cartridge that would pattern fifty percent at sea level (improved cylinder) will pattern about seventy percent (full choke) at an elevation of 7,800 feet in Pachuca.

It is also of significance that thin air at high altitudes does not slow down shot at the same rate, so that a Number 8 pellet will have about the same energy as a Number 7½ pellet produces at sea level.

Briley Screw-in Chokes

Another innovation of high-technology machining derivation is the Briley screw-in choke. These choke tubes can be fitted to any barrels, steel or Damascus, if wall thickness in the last three inches of the muzzle is sufficient. Not only are Briley tubes very efficient, but they give any gun wide flexibility in choke variations. The shooter can easily change the amount of choke to suit the day's sport.

If improving versatility is the sole objective, however, it is hard to imagine that the proud owner of a London best gun would have the heart to resort to such a solution, however technically excellent it may be. Consideration should be given, as well, to the ultimate resale value of a fine gun that has been modified in any way.

Screw-in tubes are also useful to restore choke in barrels that have been cut off or bored out, whether carelessly or purposely. If desired, they can be installed permanently and can even be well concealed.

In addition, Briley makes choke tubes that are specifically designed for steel shot. It is therefore possible for quality English shotguns to be used in America for waterfowl. If a gun is proofed for at least 1¼ ounces and weighs some 7½ pounds or more, it will make a fine waterfowl gun, whether it has Damascus or steel barrels.

If such a gun is to be used only for duck or goose shooting, changeable chokes tubes are really not needed. A reasonable choice would be a constriction of 0.005 inch in the right (or under) barrel and 0.010 inch in the left (or over) barrel. Cartridges of 2¾-inch length with $1^1/_8$ ounces of steel shot (no larger than BBs) are recommended. With such a combination, waterfowling can be enjoyed again in spite of bureaucratic interference.

✧ Chapter 6 ✧

Various

At the end of the work you may judge the workman.

– Yorkshire proverb

Various

Various is a common field shooting term in Great Britain. It is one of those appealing language shortcuts that economically defines anything shot in a day of sport not officially categorized as game, for example, magpies and carrion crows. A day's tally for a line of guns might include 600 pheasants, seven woodcocks, nineteen partridges, and eleven various.

This chapter contains various unrelated subjects concerning the English shotgun, hence the use of the term for its title. This does not imply that the various subjects are unimportant; they are simply not as fundamental as the lock, stock, and barrel. Various may also have a better ring than "miscellaneous," a term that might detract from the importance of these topics in their relationship to a best gun.

Ejectors

Hammerless guns replaced hammer guns essentially because of a faster firing cycle (*see Chapter 8*). For the same reason, ejectors were developed and perfected until they became a rather standard feature of best hammerless sidelock guns. The first ejector system was invented and patented by Needham in 1874. A series of improvements then rapidly appeared on the scene. Design and functional performance were substantially enhanced by the Southgate system of 1889 that, with only slight variation, is found on most side-by-side guns made in Britain today.

Over/under guns present an entirely different set of ejector design problems. Ejectors for these types of guns have passed through several stages since the Boss system of 1909 and the Woodward system shortly after. Current designs used by Grant, Purdey, and Holland & Holland on their sidelock over/under guns are relatively simple and reliable.

It is fair to say, however, that timesaving qualities of ejectors must be weighed against far simpler and more dependable extractors that preceded them. Reduced firing-cycle time was, and probably still is, important for driven birds. For most gameshooting situations worldwide, ejectors can actually be less desirable and can exacerbate the litter of empty cartridges on the ground or water. Sportsmen today are unquestionably more aware of this legitimate concern than they were in the past.

Single Triggers

There is a powerful temptation to dismiss the single trigger as a complex refinement of dubious value. Although this viewpoint has support from many shotgun experts, the single trigger seems to have its devotees who take strong exception and consider it critical to shooting success.

Development of a workable single trigger began in earnest just before 1900. It is fair to say that it is still in progress. Single triggers were actually attempted on many double-barrel muzzleloaders, but apparently none of them functioned satisfactorily. Early problems came from a basic misunderstanding. Gunmakers at first did not realize that shooters experience a second, involuntary trigger pull that is nearly simultaneous with firing (recoil) of the first shot. This reaction would, of course, cause the second barrel to fire unintentionally.

Modern single triggers are designed to defeat this involuntary pull by one of two methods: a three pull mechanism or a disconnecting mechanism. Both solutions require careful adjustment and suffer from two fundamental problems. First is human variation, whether it be size and build, the way the shooter holds the gun, or cartridge preference. It is a strange, but prevalent, anomaly that a particular single trigger on a given gun may not work for one individual, while functioning perfectly well for others. The second problem is a derivative of cleanliness. A speck of dirt or a drop of congealed oil can undermine careful adjustment of tiny springs, levers, and/or swinging weights found in single trigger mechanisms.

The way to avoid having this delicate mechanism at the control center of the gun is to use more reliable double triggers. If this conclusion seems biased, add the choice of choke (barrel selection) provided by double triggers. Faster performance cannot be claimed by either alternative, single or double. The case for double triggers rests at this point.

Engraving (*see Figures 30 through 33*)
Engraving has both practical and subjective (emotional) aspects. The latter is obviously personal, somewhat like art appreciation. Because of the infinite variety of styles, the beauty of engraving lies in the eyes of the beholder.

From a more practical viewpoint, physical features of the gun itself provide justification for engraving. Highly polished, flat metal surfaces simply cry out for ornamentation. Early engraving tended to represent scenes familiar to the shooter. It featured game birds, animals, or foliage, which was interpreted by scroll work. With advanced development of Damascus barrels, some British engravers stylized foliage (scroll) and made it fine, so that the flat surfaces that were compatible with the look of Damascus, which gave the gun a pleasing overall appearance (*see Figure 23, lower gun*).

The art of engraving is a good example of apprenticeship practices that are characteristic of why the quality levels of English guns remain so high. In addition to innate artistic talent, an aspiring engraver must train for many years before he can be trusted with working on a best gun. High standards set over the years by the great masters of the art, like John Sumner and Harry Kel, are upheld today by such talents as Keith Thomas, Alan and Paul Brown, and Ken Hunt.

It is not surprising that Mr. Hunt's son and daughter have both become fine engravers themselves, carrying forward their father's craft. Incidentally, the engraving art today boasts other female artisans, such as Louise Hunter of Holland & Holland. The craft is no longer the sole purview of male craftsmen.

The best engravers today must be booked at least a year or more in advance (*see Chapter 7*), and the work sometimes proceeds at glacial speed. It is, therefore, amusing to reflect on the following work order that reveals the available talent, economic circumstances, and productivity of an earlier time:

1 October 1904

Mr. John Sumner,

Please engrave in your very best manner this pair of guns No. 1674-5 for the usual price. Put on as much as you can afford. Let me have them end of next week.

– Henry Atkin

Proof

Over 350 years ago, England began testing all firearms for strength in order to protect the public. The London Proof House is the oldest in the world. It was established in 1637 under the Charter of the Worshipful Company of Gunmakers, an early trade guild. In 1813 another proof house was established in Birmingham, where many guns and muskets were being made. The Proof Act of 1868 mandated that both proof houses employ identical standards.

The basics of proof are rather straightforward. A barreled action with very smooth, straight barrels is fired with heavy overloads (proof loads). The barrels are then carefully viewed by a proof official to determine if any deformity has occurred, or if the action has bent (come off the face) or cracked. If a firearm passes proof, it is stamped with special markings that advise the public of maximum safe loads, assuming it has not been altered since time of proof. (*See the selected bibliography for references on the subject of proof marks.*)

As an example, for a 12-bore, 2¾ inch, 1¼-ounce cartridge proof, each barrel is fired with a load of approximately five drams equivalent of powder and 1¾ ounces of shot. If the gun passes this heavy overload without damage, it will be safe for all normal 1¼ ounce, 12-bore cartridges.

Proof houses of the European community have adopted a standard pressure for similar testing, but the London Proof House continues to represent the highest world standard because of the critical eyes of the proof officials. American guns are not subject to proof testing.

Care and Maintenance

Like any mechanical device, guns require reasonable care and maintenance. Even with such care, some minor failures or breakdowns are to be expected over many years of use. Best guns are designed to permit easy replacement of those parts that eventually fail with time and use.

For example, springs and strikers (firing pins) will break. Hinge (cross) pins and cuts in the lumps (hooks and bites) become worn. Ribs and fore-end loops may loosen. All of these minor maladies can be easily repaired, like a new set of tires or a carburetor overhaul on an automobile. Blacking of metal parts wears off at points of friction after much use and a stock's smooth surface and finish may require reworking. Again, redoing such finishing work may be compared to repainting a fine car.

Intervals between minor repairs can be lengthened by proper care and maintenance of a gun.

Lubrication: When a gun is assembled each time for use, a drop of high-quality oil or grease should be put on the hook (hinge pin) of side-by-sides or the trunions of over/unders to ease the rotation of barrels and to reduce wear. All bearing surfaces of the lumps benefit from lubrication as well, as do surfaces where the fore-end and action knuckle join. Points of wear normally manifest themselves as shiny spots caused by rubbing. The recommended locations for lubrication are illustrated in Figure 34.

During periods when a gun is not in use, a light coating of oil should be applied externally with care that no oil penetrates the critical union of wood to metal through striker (firing pin) holes, trigger slots, or cocking lever openings. The chance of this happening is more likely when spray cans of oil are used for this purpose. If possible, a gun should be stored muzzle down to ensure that traces of oil do not enter the open grain of the buttstock.

It is also recommended that the action of a fine gun be dismantled (stripped), inspected and cleaned thoroughly by a qualified gunsmith at least every two years or so, more often when used extensively in bad weather. Shooters are advised not to do this themselves.

Relief of Springs: When a hammerless gun is not to be used for a week or so and is to be dismantled for case storage, the main springs should be relieved (uncocked). To accomplish this end, the owner should never snap the triggers on an empty chamber. Some form of resistance to the forward movement of the strikers (firing pins) should be provided to prevent damage, since strikers are not designed to be snapped unresisted in this manner.

Two safe methods are recommended:

1. Load the gun with proper snap caps and pull both triggers to snap the locks. Remove the fore-end, which will prevent the fall of the barrels from recocking the tumblers (hammers). Remove the barrels from the action and drop out the snap caps.

2. With the barrels and fore-end off the action, place the breech firmly against a block of hard wood or plastic and pull the riggers to snap the locks. The strikers should leave a mark on the block.

This procedure is not necessary on an Atkin or a Purdey spring opener (Beesley patent), since the main springs are not compressed until the gun is closed. The springs are relieved when the gun is dismantled. If any gun is to be stored in an assembled mode, snap caps should be used to relieve the main springs, and the gun should be stored upright with the muzzles down.

Closing a Gun: Often the worst abuse a gun receives is the manner in which it is repeatedly closed. Most shooters do not realize the damage they inflict by slamming shut or even vigorously closing their guns. It is totally unnecessary.

No gun, however well designed, can accommodate the stress on the hinge pin and locking system that is caused by slamming a gun shut. It will rapidly loosen and then require repair. On the other hand, a gun closed properly will function for decades, regardless of heavy use. Shotguns are designed for repeated firing, but not for the leveraged stress of banging closures.

A gun should always be closed firmly but slowly, much like closing a heavy door with a stained glass window panel. Similarly, with hammer guns, which do not cock on opening, care should be taken to open the gun slowly, so the lumps and/or hinge pins are not stressed by an unresisted stop.

Spring opening guns (such as Atkins and Purdeys) and assisted opening guns are somewhat difficult to close. The following technique of closing is useful: After loading in an upright position, rotate the still opened gun about 80 degrees so that the underside of the buttstock rests against your waist or hip and is held firmly with your right hand. Use the forward left hand to push the underside of the barrels *slowly* away from your body to close the gun. Little effort is required.

A safety precaution: When closing any gun, be sure the muzzle is pointing in a safe direction at the moment the breech is closed. It is at this instant that a jammed firing pin or a malfunctioning or dirty sear could cause the gun to discharge accidentally.

In the same vein, a closed hammer gun should always be pointed upward (at 45 to 80 degrees) in a safe direction before cocking the hammers. The thumb should be placed resolutely across the hammer spur when cocking. To unload a hammer gun, it is procedurally safer to open the breech before letting down the hammers. These hammer gun precautions are advisable in spite of the inherent built-in safety of the half cock (*see Chapter 8*).

Transporting Guns: A handcrafted, well-fitting gun case is not only a handsome complement to a fine gun, but serves to protect it as well. A gun should be dismantled and placed in its protective case before any travel of appreciable distance. It takes only a little banging contact to dent a barrel or stock, and many a stock has been broken because of shifting luggage when a gun was transported in a soft case.

Airline travel is especially hazardous. Rough handling has been perfected to a science by most carriers. Special cases made of hard and durable plastic or aluminum can be fitted to any gun with secure ties and blocks, a precaution not usually needed for auto transport. For air travel, some shooters prefer to pack their gun in its usual hard case, and then surround it with clothing in a duffel bag. This procedure, while effective, carries with it the inconvenience of producing the gun for inspection at check in.

SIMPLIFIED FLOW CHART
MAKING A LONDON BEST GUN

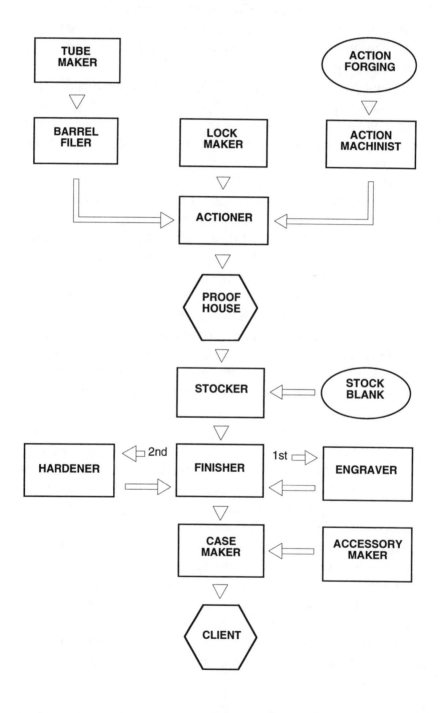

✤ Chapter 7 ✤
Making a London Best Gun – The Process

Let us have a look at what the manufacture of a good gun means, and at the same time bear in mind that it is in every detail constructed with as much care and accuracy as the fittings of a valuable watch.

– Sir Ralph Payne-Gallwey

Nature of the Process

Tracing the process of making a London best gun is a revealing exercise. Few people outside the trade are familiar with the tortuous steps that take place between the initial order and delivery of the finished gun in its custom case. It is not common knowledge among shooters, either, that making these fine guns requires the special skills of eleven expert craftsmen, plus many other skilled workmen.

Although some outstanding artisans are qualified to perform two or more roles in the process, other practical issues like shop equipment, tools, jigs, and templates enter the picture. Separation of each stage of work is therefore favored to perform the specialized skills required for each phase of the process.

The process presented here is a brief overview of the steps taken from the time the gunmaker takes an order to its ultimate delivery. In the interest of a simplified description, some side paths have not been included and mention is not made of numerous divisions, forks, and returns that some parts of a gun make as the process unfolds. This abridgment of detail is undertaken to make it easier to focus on the basic flow of work in gunmaking. In addition, no attempt is made to cover the details of how the work is performed, but even this abbreviated description should make it easier to understand why it takes two or three years to schedule the work and produce a finished gun. A simplified flow chart at the conclusion of the text further summarizes the process.

This presentation does make it clear that each gun is individually crafted to meet the unique specifications of its future owner. The question is often asked: Why do handmade English guns look and feel so much better than standardized machine made guns? The answer, for the most part, is that components can be tailored to the owner's preference. It is the hallmark of a best gun. Only by skilled hand work can the best balance and feel be met for a set of specifications.

In this space age of manufacturing by computer-driven tools and procedures, it is difficult to imagine a sophisticated product still made by hand. Perhaps the nature of the process can be understood by a breakdown of the approximate man-hours involved. A London best gun with a normal amount of engraving requires in the neighborhood of 1,200 man-hours to produce.

The following rough breakdown of the total man-hours by phases is a reasonable estimate:

> 1. Initial phase—about 40%
>   Make locks, machine body, make tubes, and then join barrels, file action and proof.
>
> 2. Stocking phase—about 15%
>   File up iron work and furniture and then stock, including fore-end.
>
> 3. Engraving phase—about 20%
>   Prepare for engraving and engrave.
>
> 4. Final phase—about 25%
>   Color harden, fully finish, and regulate, plus case and accessories.

How does this expenditure of time relate to cost? Hourly rates obviously vary for different craftsmen, and engraving, for example, is usually done on a piece basis. A 1995 range of £15 to £20 ($25 to $33) per hour is not an unreasonable estimate. These numbers clearly demonstrate that the excellence of the results comes at a corresponding price. Obviously, material costs represent a relatively small percentage of the total, even though a good French walnut blank may cost £1,000 and only the finest metals are used to make these guns.

This breakdown of man-hours does not track precisely the production steps presented in more detail below. It will be of more interest to examine the work flow of individual craftsmen in the making of best guns. How, then, does the making of the gun unfold?

The Initial Steps

The process begins, of course, with an order. The gunmaker must have a thorough understanding of the wishes of the buyer, who may or may not require assistance in arriving at specifications for the gun he wants. In some cases, a trip to the shooting grounds is advisable to confirm matters such as fit.

As a minimum, the following issues must be resolved: bore, type of action, length of barrels, top rib shape, chokes (for specified cartridge load), finished weight and point of balance, stock dimensions and configuration, engraving type and coverage, and case type, accessories, and spare parts.

In possession of these data, the gunmaker must orchestrate the entire process. He orders chopper lump tubes to the desired length and rough, undersized bore diameter. The tube maker rifle-drills the forgings and then grinds them to the approximate outside contours that the gunmaker has stipulated. This work is done using a full-length, contoured revolving stone and templates.

When rough chopper lump tubes are delivered, they pass into the hands of the barrel filer. He and the gunmaker decide on the final thickness of the barrels and ribs that in combination will produce the specified weight and balance. The barrel filer is now prepared to undertake a task requiring remarkable skill-striking off the barrels.

The process involved is a challenge to one's credibility. The barrel filer uses a succession of striking irons to remove excess steel until the shape and thickness are precisely correct. It is difficult to imagine the skill required to maintain the hole (bore) perfectly in the center of these remarkably thin tubes.

The barrels are joined by brazing, and the ribs are attached by tinning. The whole is then struck up properly and polished with emery cloth to a finely contoured perfection. Later in the process, barrels will be chambered, fine bored, choked, and lapped to final internal dimensions.

Meanwhile, the gunmaker has instructed his lock maker to produce a pair of locks of his specified design, and he has ordered a solid action forging that is delivered to the action machinist. It is the assignment of the action machinist, using the gunmaker's jigs and templates, to produce a rough, machined action body with the necessary internal cavities and passageways to accommodate his proprietary mechanism.

The gunmaker, having satisfied himself that the components are nearly perfect in every respect, delivers the barrels, locks, and machined action body to the actioner.

From Actioner to Stocker

The job of the actioner might be thought of as an assembling and fitting function of critical importance. The mechanical integrity and performance of the gun rely on his skills and are his responsibility. First, he must fit barrels and locks to the action body. Then he files up and installs the internal parts, fore-end iron and ejectors, triggers, trigger guard, and opening lever. These components are often referred to as the furniture of the gun. They are made by the actioner. He must also file the outside of the action to the shape and weight specified by the gunmaker.

After the gunmaker carefully measures and inspects the work to ensure that the gun, now in the white, has proper integrity and shape, the locks, fore-end iron and trigger plate are removed, leaving only the barreled action, which is delivered to the London Proof House. Here the gun is tested for strength with heavy test load charges (*see Chapter 6*). If it passes this rigorous proof, it is permanently marked as safe for use, unless it is altered.

The gun is then reassembled in the white for delivery to the stocker. A stock blank was chosen by the gunmaker, who selected it from his prized inventory. The stocker saws an outline of the stock profile from the block of French walnut and hopes to discover at this early stage any hidden defects. A highly figured blank is wonderfully desirable, but notoriously unpredictable. One serious defect at the wrong spot renders the costly blank useless.

The stocker heads the roughly measured stock by fitting the front end (head) of the stock to the rear of the action, which is accomplished by repeated trials, cutting adjustments, and smoke tests (to pinpoint any irregularities). It is critical that intimate fit of head to action be precise and true, because this interface must continuously withstand the stress transfer of recoil from metal to wood (*see Figures 26a and 26b*).

Once satisfied with this important aspect, the stocker must then perform the delicate task of inletting to accept the locks and trigger plate, adjusting them as required. It is a tribute both to his skill and to the innate properties of French walnut that this work can be accomplished with such close tolerances. Although not externally apparent, locks fit so snugly into the stock that lock component screws will not back out even a part of a turn because the heads are in firm contact with the wood (*see Figure 25*). Wood to external metal fit of a London best gun can be appreciated not only by experts, but by anyone who examines it closely.

Other tasks of the stocker are to fit the fore-end wood to the iron and to finish shaping the buttstock to exact contours and dimensions. For these tasks, he uses his practiced eye, as well as templates to assure that the finished shape is precisely as it was specified. Throughout each phase of the work, there is the ever present danger that a flaw in the wood will manifest itself and cause the job to be scrapped and started over.

The last chore is to lay out the checkering pattern. (The actual checkering is normally done by the finisher.) It is a determining characteristic of best guns that checkering on both sides of the wrist will join at the top and bottom without a flaw, a most difficult accomplishment.

Finishing Steps

The gun, stocked in the white, now goes to the finisher, a highly versatile and skilled artisan. His many tasks include completing the screws (pins) that purposely have been left long. He cuts slots in the heads so that all of them will line up the same, making it possible for the owner to judge at a glance if one has become loose. He hones, fits, and polishes all the metal parts until the gun functions perfectly and is shootable, although it is still soft. Wood components are then removed and metal parts are ready for the engraver.

The gunmaker and the engraver must confer and decide on exactly the type and amount of engraving work to be done. As with other artists of reputation, the engraver sets about performing his task in his own way and at his own speed. Work can cover many months of off-and-on effort, depending upon artistic whim and impetus, but it usually proceeds at a rate that causes the gunmaker great despair. In addition, fine work of the best engravers is in such demand that they must be booked a year or more in advance.

When the gunmaker ultimately accepts the engraving work, he delivers the gun back to the finisher, who must now repolish and refit anything that has gone amiss at the engraver's workshop. He then completely dismantles the gun and sends the action, lock plates, fore-end iron and trigger plate to the hardener.

The hardener cleans these parts and separates them into different size groupings for the hardening process. The basics of this process consist of placing a group of parts in a bed of special carbonaceous material (such as charcoal and bone meal) and slowly heating it to the required temperature. Metal surfaces react by absorbing extra carbon, which produces an incredibly hard skin. After a proper time at the right temperature, parts are removed, quenched in a water bath, immediately dried, and varnished.

The hardened parts are returned to the finisher, who must at this point address any warping and distortion that resulted from heating and cooling. This work is complicated by the fact that the metal now has such a hard skin it cannot be cut with a file and must therefore be worked with a stone. Metal parts are again finished, and the gun is restored to perfect working order.

Sometime during the finishing phase, the barrels were sent out to be blackened, by the process described in Chapter 2. It is also the job of the finisher to blacken the remaining small items (furniture), polish the buttstock and fore-end, checker the wood, fill pores, administer the correct amount of stain, and apply numerous coats of oil finish (*see Chapter 4 for details*).

The gunmaker, who has inspected and accepted work at every step, now receives the gun from the finisher, and test fires it for choke, point of impact, and mechanical perfection, some, or all, of which may need slight alterations. After adjustments are made, he takes the finished gun to the case maker, who crafts a case that meets order requirements and houses the gun with tailored exactitude. Although cases may vary substantially in price, depending upon the materials used and other features, all may be counted upon to fulfill the expectation of a good fit. Accessories, as ordered, are provided by the accessory maker, himself no mean craftsman.

A normal set of accessories includes: a complete cleaning kit with wooden or ebonite rod and various tips; snap caps for testing triggers and ejectors and for relieving the main springs before storage; a thin, steel-frame, leather-covered hand guard to protect the forward hand from hot barrels; and an oil bottle with an applicator to apply lubrication to wear points before assembly.

At this point, the finished gun, in its custom case with accessories and spare parts, is ready for delivery to the client. Elapsed time from order to delivery is normally in the range of two to three years, which should be understandable considering the steps described above and the critical scheduling difficulties that are inherent in such a complicated process. The flow chart that follows is a graphic representation of the process, showing the eleven interrelated craftsmen whose constituent skills are essential to the production of a London best gun.

SIMPLIFIED FLOW CHART
MAKING A LONDON BEST GUN

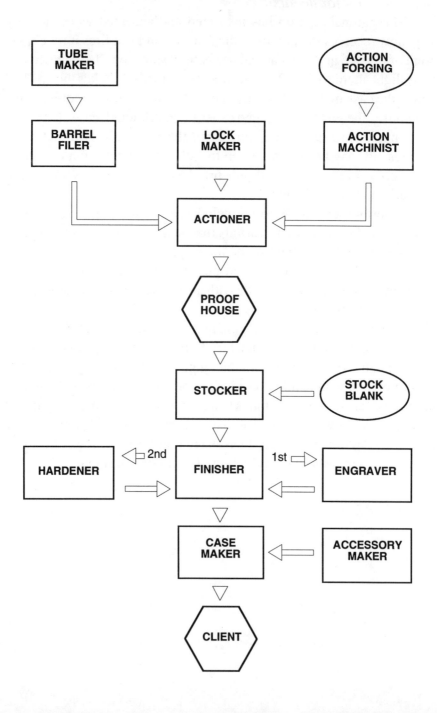

✛ Chapter 8 ✛

The Hammer Gun

Excellent things are rare.

– Plato

Hammer Gun Era

Breechloading, center-fire, and side-by-side shotguns, balanced and shaped as we know them today, were first made with external hammers and no ejectors. Modern hammer guns came on the scene during the 1870s and were made only rarely after 1900. Thus, the Golden Age of the modern hammer gun was only about twenty odd years.

During this interesting period when hammer guns reigned supreme, boxlock systems were in early production. Toward the end of the period, hammerless sidelocks became the preferred choice for their comparable excellence. For several critical years, though, all best guns had external hammers.

The modern hammer gun represented a natural evolution of gun design. In the case of the earlier flintlocks, hammers had jaws to hold replaceable flints. Percussion guns, on the other hand, had cupped hammers to contain cap fragments. They were soon followed by pinfire guns, which had hammers centrally located to strike the top of the breech end of the barrels. Here the firing pins (integral to the cartridges) protruded upward. Finally, in center-fire guns, hammers were relocated to strike permanent firing pins (strikers) located in the breech of the action body. The firing pins in turn struck the cartridge primer.

Shooters of this era, then, were always accustomed to some type of external hammers. In fact, percussion, pinfire, and center-fire guns were all seen in the field until the late 1800s. It is interesting to reflect that a little over 100 years ago the best available guns were hammer guns, which would suggest that they belong in a bygone area. To the contrary, there has recently been a renaissance in the use of these splendid pieces among a dedicated coterie of shooters, who can advance persuasive arguments that hammer guns are preeminent even today.

The Safety Issue

None of the hammer guns, as shotguns, had safety catches. As rifles though, they often had catches to hold the hammers, a feature that was justifiable when stalking game in dense brush. Modern hammer guns do not require safety catches, and yet they are inherently safe because of a simple design conceived and patented by John Stanton in 1867–the rebounding lock.

Before this improvement, hammers on flintlocks, percussion, pinfire, and center-fire guns remained where they fell. In the case of center-fire guns, this down position was undesirable because it left the point of the striker projecting through the breech face and into the cartridge primer, with the hammer face hard against the butt of the striker. A fired gun, with non-rebounding hammers, is difficult to open without manually placing the hammer on one-half cock, because striker points must be forced back out of the dents in the cartridge primers. It can be done inadvertently, however, in the excitement of fast shooting action, which in turn may cause an accidental discharge when the chambers are reloaded and the action is closed. For this reason, very old hammer guns with non-rebounding locks (hammers) should either be converted or retired from use.

Ironically, Stanton's rebounding system was immediately accepted and warmly embraced, not so much as a safety improvement, but primarily because it speeded the firing cycle. It was now unnecessary to bring hammers to half cock manually. Stanton's system was soon adopted by all makers.

Those shooters unfamiliar with modern hammer guns (with rebounding hammers) often express skepticism about the safety of a gun without a trigger-blocking device, or safety. Such concern is unwarranted. According to many experts, the half-cock notch that is automatically engaged on a hammer gun is actually preferable to the later trigger-blocking devices of hammerless guns.

When the barrels of a hammer gun are closed and the sears are in the half-cock notch (hammers down), the gun is truly safe because it will not fire when the triggers are pulled or if the gun is accidentally dropped. In contrast, a hammerless gun is fully cocked when closed. The internal hammers are simply not visible.

Even when the hammers are back and in mode for firing, the hammer gun will not fire when dropped. If the sear is jarred out of its notch or bent, the hammer will fall only partway to the half-cock notch, which is not the case for the vast majority of hammerless guns today. (High quality sidelocks and a rare boxlock can duplicate this safety feature by adding an intercepting sear to the lock, but it is costly and difficult to adjust.) Even if the thumb slips off the hammer in cocking, it will fall only to the half-cock notch position and prevent an accidental discharge.

Still, there are those who remain uncomfortable with hammer guns that have no trigger safety to disengage immediately before pulling the trigger. The answer to this concern, of course, lies in the irrefutable proposition that no gun is truly safe that is not pointing in a safe direction. Reliance on a trigger safety is a false sense of security that is the probable cause of many accidents in the field. A safety should never be trusted.

It is interesting, however, that a few pairs of late hammer guns were equipped with automatic safeties. This anomaly probably resulted from the sad experiences of driven-bird shooters who were using hammerless guns that cocked automatically. In the excitement of a big drive, loaders on rare occasions pulled a trigger accidentally, which was obviously a problem inherent in employing a pair of guns, whether hammer or hammerless. In the case of hammer guns, danger existed only if the loader had instructions to cock the hammers, an option that shooters apparently seldom elected.

The Transition Period

During the 1880 to 1890 decade, several best makers began producing hammerless guns, as well as classic hammer guns. The increasing popularity of this innovation was based squarely on the perception that the firing cycle was speeded, since internal hammers were cocked automatically either by the opening lever or by the movement of the barrels as the gun was opened after firing.

Around 1890, cartridge ejector systems were developed enough to be dependable, a feature that further cut cycle time. By the late 1890s, most new best guns were made as hammerless ejectors, because they were considered to be the epitome of a rapid firing gun. This reputation is deserved and has endured to the present time.

It is a matter of record, therefore, that after 1900 only a limited number of people placed orders for best-quality hammer guns. Sadly, many elegant hammer guns passed into the hands of secondary owners who did not fully appreciate them or bother to care for them properly.

Of significance, however, is the fact that several of the famous game shots of the twentieth century had pairs or even trios of hammer ejector game guns made for them into the 1920s. This circle of distinction included King George V and Lord Ripon. At the other end of the weight spectrum, best-quality hammer guns lived on in live pigeon rings, where shotgun excellence is self-proving. Select notable shooters, including some Americans and King Alphonso XIII of Spain, continued to have hammer pigeon guns made well into the 1920s (*see Figure 13*).

Hammer Gun Renaissance

For at least two decades after World War II, hammer guns languished in the back rooms of gunmakers, dealers, and private owners. Fortunately, a reasonable number of best-quality pieces stubbornly survived, even though the demand had declined to a point that supported little market value. Then, over a period of years, starting in the 1970s, these marvelous guns were rediscovered. Recognition of hammer gun excellence was gradual at first, but it gained momentum in the 1980s and has continued to the present.

Somewhat curiously, it was the American gun trade that can largely be credited with this renaissance. For a number of reasons—cost, instant availability from inventory, and perhaps novelty-English hammer guns increasingly found their way across the Atlantic, gained acceptance and recognition based on performance. More and more discerning sportsmen and a few competitive live pigeon shooters learned that the past 120 years have not produced a shotgun that has all the intrinsic qualities of the hammer gun.

Certain physical aspects should first be examined. Consider the maxim steeped in tradition and validated by experience: "A shotgun should, with few exceptions, be balanced about the hinge pin." This rather fundamental principle applies to both hammer guns and their hammerless successors. Then there is balance, and then there is real balance.

When hammers are concealed in hammerless guns, the action body must necessarily be larger both in width and depth. In fact, it must be significantly larger. The larger action changes the dimensions of the head of the stock and the relation of the trigger hand to the bore of the barrels. In addition, the hollow hammerless action is lighter than the solid hammer gun for guns of comparable size, which means that the stock and barrels must be made heavier to attain a prescribed weight. This weight distribution is a movement away from the hands as opposed to between them, which detracts from the liveliness of the gun.

Although some may argue that this distribution change would be noticed only by the most discerning of shooters, there is actually a different mounting and swinging feel to a fine hammer gun. It is often described as sweeter. It is apparent that this feel derives from the weight resting more between the hands.

Hammer guns, because of weight-design flexibility, can also accommodate longer barrels more easily. Because of the design flexibility, hammer guns also point and swing more effectively, in the opinion of many shooting authorities. Latitude to make weight adjustments, whether in distribution or in total weight, is a function of action design. Even 12-bore hammer-gun actions can be filed down small and yet remain strong because there are fewer internal parts and required passageways to accommodate them, compared to hammerless guns.

The celebrated durability and dependability of hammer guns is also a by-product of simplicity and fewer parts. Many late model hammer guns were made for sportsmen who were off to Africa or other primitive areas on extended safaris or assignments. For this type of service, rugged, dependable guns with easily replaceable parts (mostly strikers and main springs) counted for much more than the faster firing cycle of a hammerless gun.

Still another pleasant feature of the nonejector hammer gun is ease of opening and closing. The barrels open by themselves since they are not used as levers to cock the locks, as is the case with most hammerless guns. Closing is also smoothly uninterrupted because the barrels, once again, are not called upon to act as levers to cock ejectors. Only those hammerless guns using the Beesley patent of 1880, made today by Atkin and Purdey, open by themselves. Even then, the closing cycle is a bit awkward and difficult, though less so for the Atkin.

In addition to the positive physical advantages cited above, it is also entirely reasonable to conclude that best-quality hammer guns are the most elegant and beautifully proportioned guns ever made. From the standpoint of aesthetics, many, if not most gun experts would agree that the hammer gun is the ultimate sporting gun.

Its long, lean profile is interrupted only by the artistic hammers themselves, which serve as dramatic highlights. Slim barrels seem to flow into the elongated, shallow action. Delicate lines of the action are matched by the gracile wrist of the stock, which is pleasing to the eye as well as the hand. These elegant lines are approached by the hammerless sidelock, but never fully attained by it or any other gun. In the minds of its votaries, there can be only one quintessential shotgun, and it is the hammer gun, which is truly the archetype of guns as an art form.

Hammer guns were made in a wonderful variety of shapes: the lovely wood bar (*see Figure 10*), the elegant round body, (*see Figure 5*), and the modern bar action (*see Figure 14*). The hammers themselves were crafted in different styles and shapes (*see Figure 23*). Lock plate configurations were individually designed, as were carved fences of astonishing grace and workmanship (*see Figures 7 and 11*). Hammerless sidelock ejectors, while handsome in their own right, are confined to a more standard shape, with only the maker's special style to distinguish them from one another.

Remarkably, the renaissance of hammer guns has not yet been fully recognized in the marketplace. They are reasonably priced. Except for pigeon guns, which bring about the same price as hammerless equivalents, a best hammer gun will cost only about sixty percent of what a comparable sidelock ejector costs. This disparity is difficult to explain and will probably vanish with time. It is based, most likely, on an irrational fear of old guns and the usual absence of ejectors. Both are poor reasons for overlooking the performance characteristics and classic elegance of the hammer gun.

In these times, particularly in America, an extractor gun may actually be considered an asset, as more and more conscientious sportsmen are loath to leave spent plastic cartridges on the ground as a nonbiodegradable reminder of thoughtlessness. Ejectors make it more inconvenient to recover empty shells.

Since hammer guns are less expensive, shooters are more likely to customize these guns and thus make them more useful. For example, sleeving barrels to create a thirty-two-inch target or dove gun somehow seems less sacrilegious to some than altering a very expensive best sidelock ejector. Similarly, to some owners, installing screw-in chokes seems a more viable option on a shooter hammer gun than on a sidelock ejector that costs twice as much. This feeling is not universal, however, and is not shared by most hammer-gun devotees.

The hammer gun renaissance has a firm basis in the features of balance, feel, safety, performance, dependability, aesthetics, and economy. Is there another ingredient to be considered? Without a question there is, but it may defy logical description. It deals with the pure pleasure afforded the shooter by certain intangibles. How does one define the feel of a hammer spur and the sound of the sear clicking into its notch as the gun is manually armed before taking a high quartering pheasant or stepping up to the dogs?

There is an indescribable sense of involvement that brings extra joy to the moment. Shooting a hammer gun compares to driving a stick-shift Ferrari up a winding mountain road. Through your hands, you are physically connected to the engine and to the entire experience. Shooting a fine hammerless ejector compares to traveling the same road in the back seat of a Mercedes with your driver at the wheel. It is no small wonder that hammer guns have been reborn, leaping the span of 120 years of technological change. Perhaps some of the appeal lies in this one instance where excellence seems frozen in time, like an enduring truth.

✤ Chapter 9 ✤

Why the English Shotgun?

Quality remains long after the price is forgotten.

– Unknown

Thesis

This presentation deals only with double-barrel guns. By and large, the text is further limited to side-by-side doubles. Finally, the history, observations, and discussion presented here refer almost exclusively to English shotguns. Why? Consider these statements:

1. The finest shotguns ever produced were made in Britain.

2. Whether new or used, the highest quality in double-barrel shotguns available for purchase today is an English gun.

3. Arguably, side-by-side doubles are the most perfectly suited game guns, when all features of performance are taken into account.

No doubt there will be readers who do not agree with all three statements, particularly the third. Most knowledgeable experts in the gun trade would, however, be able to accept each. Perhaps the paragraphs that follow will answer the question, "Why the English Shotgun?" if the chapters before this one have not already answered it.

London Best

Many shotguns of high quality have been and still are produced in Britain. The very best of these guns, with few exceptions, have been made in London, hence the origin of the term London best. Of the many London makers, only four-Boss, Grant, Purdey and Woodward-made only best guns in the normal course of business. (A few exceptions were made on rare occasions.)

Other fine gunmakers were, and are, quite capable of producing a best gun, but would make a more ordinary gun to match the weight of a buyer's purse. Quite a few London makers never produced a best gun, and many London gun shops had their guns made in Birmingham, even though the address shown on the barrels was London. Only the informed judgment of an expert can establish if the quality of a gun merits classification as best. All best guns were not made in London, but the vast majority were.

Owners of best guns share a rare privilege. They have temporary custody of and the opportunity to enjoy a practical and enduring work of art. Whether a shooter buys an older best gun or commissions a London maker to create a new one, he can be assured that with reasonable care and maintenance the gun will survive his lifetime and can be passed on for use by subsequent generations. Solid evidence of this conclusion is the number of marvelously conditioned best guns in useful service today that were made well over a hundred years ago. Clearly, best guns have been made over the years for a single reason: To meet the demanding requirements of shooters who appreciate quality and functional perfection.

Workmanship and Materials

Breechloading English guns have always been made by artisans who benefited from a preceding century or more of trial and error. Gunmaking skills have been passed from one generation to the next through a rigid apprenticeship system. It is little understood in the world of modern manufacturing, particularly not in America where few parallels exist.

Over the long history of English gunmaking, each novice struggled through the system as an apprentice before he could hope to master a part of the art that fit his unique skills and temperament. As an example, consider the names of some of the apprentices or craftsmen at Joseph and John Manton's London shops: William Greener, James Purdey, William Moore, Thomas Boss, and Charles Lancaster.

In addition, gunmakers were a close-knit group. Henry Atkin, Senior, was James Purdey's first workman in 1814 and labored in his shop for fifty years. Henry Atkin, the younger, was apprenticed to his father at Purdey's for ten years. Joseph Lang married James Purdey's daughter. Frederick Beesley and William Evans both worked for James Purdey, the younger, and Stephen Grant was the managing partner of Boss.

Even today in shops of the best makers, young apprentices are assigned to sharpening and making tools and setting up jigs and fixtures long before they make a part or work on a piece. Most of their early efforts end up in the garbage. In other locations or countries, new workers receive brief training and then begin producing guns of relatively low quality from soft, easy-to-work material. The best of them graduate to work on better grades of guns. If they show an unusual aptitude, they may end up in London, as their predecessors have in the past.

Free market economics played its part. Highest wages for skilled artisans in Britain were paid in London, so the best workmen usually ended up there and assured that the quality of the London guns would exceed that from other locations. In turn, the world's most discerning and wealthy buyers came to London to be fitted for their individually crafted guns. Fierce competition between top makers served to escalate the level of excellence.

It is also well known in the gun trade that almost all British guns, no matter where or how they were produced or how plain they may be, are made of high-quality steel and wear exceptionally well.

Internal Finish

One of the most distinguishing features of a best gun is often overlooked by the casual observer, and even by owners of fine English shotguns: All of the internal surfaces will be highly polished and notably free of tool marks and surface irregularities. Very few other guns made throughout the world give such care to internal finish, which is hidden, or partially hidden, to the eye of the beholder.

Some clue to this important aspect of quality can be seen by opening the breech and inspecting observable surfaces of the action, barrels, lumps and ejectors. Further, if the gun is dismantled by a gunsmith, exposing the internals of the locks, bolting system and ejector mechanism, the same consistency of polished excellence will be found.

These bright surfaces are usually never seen by the owner, but this added polishing effort is not just for beauty, or to prove that it can be done. Indeed, it serves a very real purpose. The extremely smooth internal finish ensures there is no place for rust to take hold. The lock maker, action filer and finisher all have a hand in grinding, filing, polishing (with emery cloth) and often burnishing the surfaces with a hard steel tool until mirror bright. This time-consuming and difficult process tends to close the pores on the surface of the steel, actually making it difficult for corrosion to find a starting point.

If the owner will simply send his gun to a competent gunsmith every other year or so for a strip and clean (the interval depending upon weather conditions to which it has been subjected), the internal parts will remain rust-free forever. Proof of this statement: A number of well maintained best muzzleloaders have survived over two centuries with their internal finish as bright and functional as the day the guns were completed.

Availability

A glaring misconception about best English guns has to do with availability. In fact, relatively few were ever made. From the time the breechloader became dominant in the late 1870s until the present, approximately 60,000 London best shotguns have been produced, according to the actual records of the gunmakers. If another 10,000 best guns were made in the rest of Britain, the total production during 120 years approaches a mere 70,000.

Of this total, about thirty percent were hammer guns. When hammerless ejectors largely replaced hammer guns in the field, most of these marvelous pieces ended up in the hands of youngsters, poor relations, or gamekeepers, where they often did not fare well. Roughly seventy-five percent of best guns were made prior to 1950, when the use of noncorrosive primers became widespread. Earlier corrosive primers often attacked barrels and breech faces, unless extreme care was exercised in cleaning them. Then, as now, such care was often lacking.

It would therefore be reasonable to estimate that at least 50 percent of the 70,000 best guns were destroyed by neglect, accidents, or loss during the last 120 years. The remaining 35,000 best guns of Britain are almost entirely in private hands around the world, with the exception of a few held by gun dealers and museums.

New best guns are being made in Britain today at the rate of less than a hundred a year, a number limited primarily by the scarcity of qualified craftsmen. Restoration of older guns accounts for some additional availability; however, this paltry rate of new production and restoration will not even match the rate of attrition, much less growing demand.

As an interesting American comparison, Parker produced approximately 240,000 shotguns after 1880, and Ithaca made 450,000 double-barrel guns. It is reasonable to assume that only thirty percent would be classified as better guns, for a combined total of 200,000. The fifty percent attrition rate is probably applicable for these American guns and suggest that about 100,000 survive today. Winchester made around 35,000 of their Model 21 double-barrel guns after World War II. Therefore, some seventy-five percent of these guns, or 26,000, should still be in service. Add another 24,000 surviving shotguns of better quality made by L. C. Smith, Fox, and Lefever, and so on.

The total, then, of better American doubles still in existence, almost all of which are in North America, might be in the range of 150,000, as compared to the remaining 35,000 best guns of Britain, which are distributed worldwide. Numbers do not tell the entire story, however, for it is impossible to support parity in quality, even by those with unremitting pride in America. These numbers do help, however, to explain the very high cost of a best English shotgun.

Price is even more understandable when the enormous time required of highly skilled craftsmen to make a single gun, about 1,200 man-hours, is considered. The high quality of specialty materials used is another factor to consider. It is no wonder that the cost of these guns has been rising continuously since World War II, and there is a strong likelihood this trend will continue.

Comparison with Continental Guns

Shooters considering the purchase of a fine shotgun are often faced with the dilemma of buying an English gun or a handsome Continental piece. It is understandable that there are disagreements over choice. There are two basic observations, or proofs, both of which favor English guns as top of the class. The first has to do with longevity. It is a common occurrence in the sporting field to encounter English guns well over a century old, still in excellent condition, still bearing up under hard service, and still the pride of their owners. The usable lifetime of a London best gun has really yet to be established. It is clearly more than 125 years.

Although a prospective buyer may be told that fine Continental shotguns are actually better than English and that some companies have been making great guns since the dawn of wingshooting, one is compelled to ask, "Where are their hundred-year-old veterans? Indeed, where are their fifty-year-old guns that are better than English guns?" The applicable law would seem to be the survival of the fittest.

The second proof has to do with sustainable value. Allegations are frequently made that new London best guns are overpriced when compared to equivalent Continental guns available at less cost, often one-half to two-thirds. Rebuttal is found in the secondhand market. A hundred-year-old London best gun will bring three to five times the price of a twenty-year-old, top of the line Continental gun at auction or in a dealer's showroom. The applicable law here is that the free market sets the value.

These observations are not meant to denigrate Continental guns or to say that fine guns are not made outside Britain. In some of the old gunmaking areas of Italy, for example, several makers produce a limited number of fine guns each year at prices approaching best English guns. They are worthy guns that merit the cost. They are not, however, London best quality-lock, stock, and barrel.

Game Guns

For the most part, English guns were made for the purpose of game shooting. Since a shotgun of light weight was considered desirable for this use, most 12-bores were produced to weigh from $6^{1}/_{2}$ to 7 pounds with an average of $6^{3}/_{4}$ pounds.

The question is often asked if there is a supportable demand for such light weight game guns in America, given the propensity for heavily loaded cartridges and the strong emphasis on clay target shooting? An examination of shotgun sport in the United States can answer this question.

The American shooting industry estimates that some 700 million clay targets were presented to shooters in 1993. Ordinarily, the 12-bore target guns used weigh between 7$^1/_4$ and 8$^1/_2$ pounds. These facts do not support much of an apparent role for English game guns. On the other hand, the United States Fish and Wildlife Service estimated that during the 1988-1989 season over 100 million upland game birds were taken by licensed shooters. It is reasonable to conclude, based on accepted cartridge-to-kill ratios, that over 400 million shells were expended by sportsmen. These numbers demonstrate that game shooting is quite significant statistically in the States, not to mention the strong appeal of the field as a shooting stage.

While it is true that most Americans who hunt game birds use target guns, the underlying reason is affordable cost. English game guns with appropriate cartridge loads are eminently suitable for those who wish to maximize their enjoyment of game shooting. Indeed, English game guns are well represented, considering their limited availability and cost.

Why Pay the Price?

Most shotguns manufactured around the world today are made with competitive low cost in mind. Though functional, these guns must be made at the sacrifice of quality and workmanship. This observation is not an indictment. Millions of shooters are beneficiaries of the availability and comparative low cost of such shotguns.

In contrast, London best guns are made with a goal of perfection in form and function. Cost scarcely enters into the picture. Producing a work of art is the goal of these gunmakers. The perfection involved in the endeavor extracts its toll. It comes as no surprise that such guns are costly, but it may not be obvious that gunmaking of this type is innately unprofitable. Not a single maker is really a business success in the production of best guns. Some have profitable related businesses.

The reason for this anomaly to basic supply and demand profitability is stubborn, yet entirely admirable, adherence to quality. Cost will not be contained at the expense of quality. As a result of the dearth of skilled artisans, few best guns can be produced. The price is high. Buyers who demand such quality and can afford the price are limited. It cannot be said that a great fortune is to be made as a London gunmaker.

On the other hand, there are compelling reasons for a buyer of means to consider investing in an English shotgun:

1. London best guns are essentially made by hand and therefore each is different, except for pairs.

2. Because of handcrafting, it is possible to give the buyer exactly what he wants. There are no standard models that cannot be altered.

3. The makers of best guns are masters of fine details and component perfection that defy today's mass production mentality.

4. When an experienced shooter picks up a best English gun, he immediately senses that it feels alive and special.

5. When anyone looks at such a shotgun, he cannot help but appreciate the smooth lines, the harmony of the components, the elegance of the engraving, and the beauty of the stock.

6. The remarkable refinements of workmanship are achieved by file and stone, not on the drawing board or by a computer mouse. A good example is the consistently smooth interior finish–not even visible to one who inspects the exterior quality only.

7. Best guns are made from several types of steel with characteristics that exactly suit the use intended, as opposed to those that suit computer-driven machining speeds or barrel-swaging machine requirements.

8. Only those materials that have proven to be the longest lasting and most trustworthy are selected to be shaped into the ingenious devices that have evolved over the past 120 years.

9. Working time from start to completion is not set. The goal is a finished product as near ideal in every way as the maker can produce.

10. Careful weight distribution, balance about the hinge pin, and a straight, slim profile contribute significantly to the wonderful feel and shooting performance of a best gun.

11. The thinness of the barrels beyond the midpoint, with the subsequent swooping profile, combined with delicate yet durable locks and action, and a stock designed to complement, also add to the incomparable feel.

12. Best guns can be made light or heavy, long or short, large or small, but all will shoot well and be astonishingly dependable (*see Figure 35*).

13. Over the decades, some parts will break on good English shotguns, but design is such that replacement is easy. Springs, strikers, hinge pins, and bolts must eventually be repaired or replaced with hard use. These elements are analogous to the spark plugs, fan belts, and tires of an automobile.

These are reasons to own and use a best English gun. Unfortunately, such quality and performance is beyond the price range of most shooters. However, the very ingredients that have given rise to the high cost establish enduring value, as with any work of art. It has often been said that one does not buy a London best gun, as he might an expensive car. He simply invests in an art form that can also provide great joy as a shooting companion for life. In the end, if properly cared for, the value should be greater than the original cost. Seldom does one encounter this sort of opportunity.

A Word of Caution

It is a sad commentary that the steadily appreciating value of English shotguns has encouraged production of false and altered guns, which are sold to the unwary as original guns or properly restored ones. Buyers should understand that there are precious few bargains at this end of the gun market. As in the case of art or other quality collectibles, one should proceed with appropriate caution.

Few individuals, and especially Americans, have sufficient background knowledge to understand fully the intricacies or veracity of proof marks, the identifying characteristics of the guns of each maker, the authenticity of original barrels, the fact that a proper or improper sleeving or restocking job has been done, the effect that any modifications may have on resale value, and many other details. Potential buyers should therefore deal only with reputable dealers and makers or seek advice from an expert. If a second opinion is justifiable in medicine, it is doubly so when investing in an English shotgun. *Caveat emptor* takes on a whole new meaning in this arena.

King George V

George V and his father, Edward VII, are sometimes referred to as England's shooting kings. Until his death in 1936, King George used hammer ejector Purdey shotguns. He owned three trios of 12-bores, and one trio of 16-bore.

Lord Ripon

Earl de Grey, born 1852, succeeded as Second Marquess of Ripon in 1909. He is reputed by many to have been the best game shot in history. He died in 1923 while shooting, after he had made a left and right on grouse. Until his death, he shot Purdey hammer guns. His last guns were a trio of hammer ejectors made in 1894-1896.

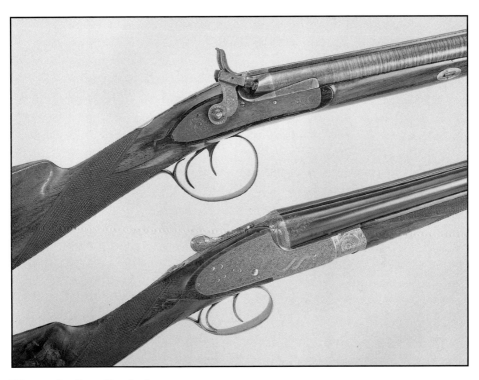

Figure 1– Gun Evolution

Upper: Manton percussion 20-bore; SN 8804; weight 6 pounds; c. 1830.
Lower: Grant center-fire 20-bore; SN 24005; weight 6 pounds; c. 1992.

These guns were made more than 160 years apart, and yet size, shape, balance, and proportion have changed very little. Joseph Manton was indeed the father of the modern shotgun.

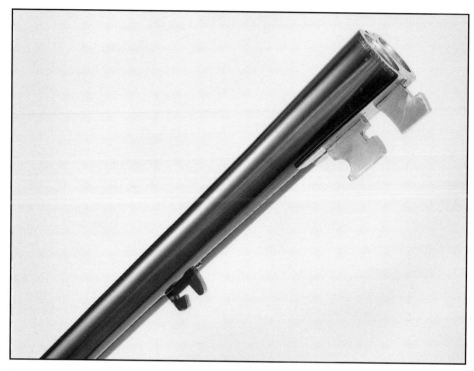

Figure 2 – Barrel Lumps

The two large projections under the breech end of the barrels are the lumps. The semicircular, forward-facing cut (or hook) fits against the hinge (or cross) pin and permits the barrels to rotate during opening or closing.

The two rectangular, rear-facing cuts (or bites) engage the Purdey sliding bolt when the barrels are snugly closed down against the action face. The flats on the under surface of the barrels match and fit the action flats with a uniform space of 0.002 to 0.005 of an inch along the length of the interface. The rear of the barrels fits perfectly on the face of the action (or standing breech).

The sides of the lumps bear against the sides of the slot in the action flat (or bar) and gives the barrels lateral stability.

The lumps may be forged integrally with the barrels (one-half to each tube), in which case they are called chopper lumps, or they may be produced separately and brazed in later, in which case they are called dovetail (through or horseshoe) lumps.

The smaller projection (more forward on the barrels) is the fore-end loop. Pictured here is the loop design to engage an Anson Push Rod type of fore-end fastener. The forward notch accepts the spring driven bolt in the fore-end and holds it securely in place against the barrels. The rear projection fits a camming surface in the fore-end iron, which forces the fore-end back against the action knuckle.

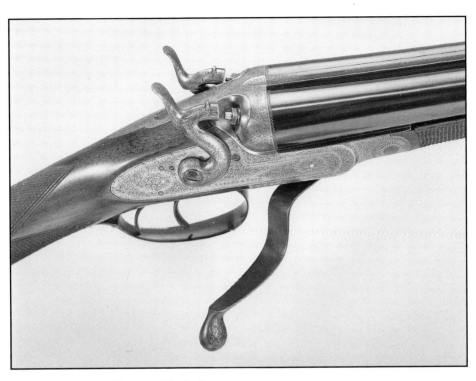

Figure 3 – Jones Rotary Underlever

Purdey hammer gun 20-bore; SN 10220; weight 6 pounds, 4 ounces; c. 1878.
In this position, the Jones Rotary Underlever is about one-half open.

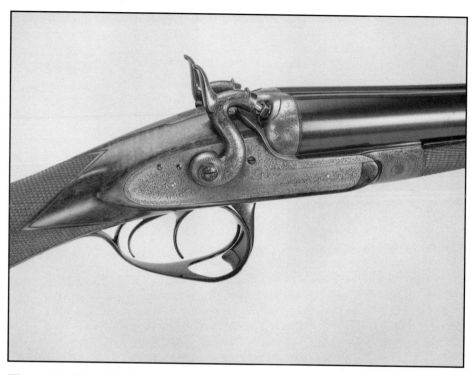

Figure 4 – Thumbhole

Purdey hammer gun 12-bore; SN 9011; weight 6 pounds, 13 ounces; c. 1872.

The thumbhole lever (second pattern) pictured here was the first operating mechanism used in conjunction with the Purdey sliding bolt. It was patented in 1863.

Figure 5 – Snap Underlever

Norman hammer gun 12-bore; SN 785; weight 6 pounds, 12 ounces; c. 1883.

This Norman snap underlever wraps around the trigger guard and gives it an extended arm with greater leverage than the thumbhole. It is convenient for right-handed or left-handed shooters. The extended top strap, well illustrated here, reinforces the wrist of the stock.

Figure 6 – Snap Underlever

Gibbs hammer gun 12-bore; SN C 367; weight 7 pounds, 3 ounces; c. 1880.

This snap underlever is turned at the terminal end, specifically to accommodate a right-handed shooter. Note the beautifully carved fences on this gun.

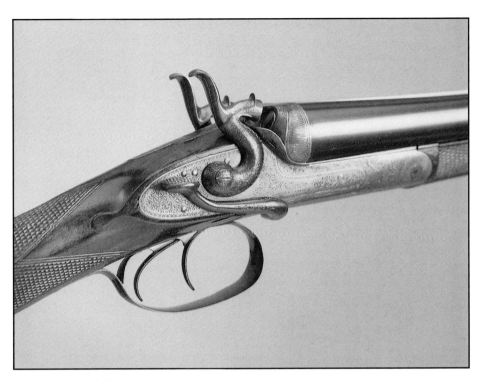

Figure 7 – Sidelever

Reilly hammer gun 12-bore; SN 20155; weight 7 pounds, 2 ounces; c. 1880.

The graceful shape and convenience of the sidelever made it very popular. It may be positioned on either side of the action.

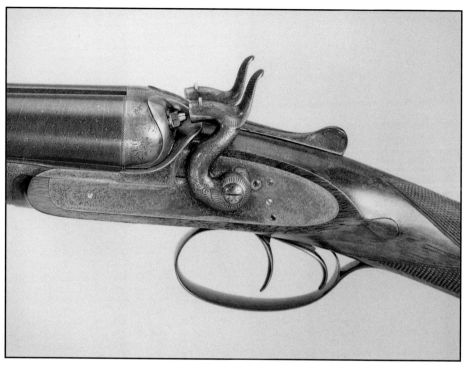

Figure 8 – Top Lever (Scott Spindle)

Purdey hammer gun 20-bore; SN 10734; weight 5 pounds, 4 ounces; c. 1879.

The top lever (Scott spindle) has become the most common way to engage the Purdey sliding bolt in side-by-side guns, as well as the basis for various operating mechanisms of over/under guns.

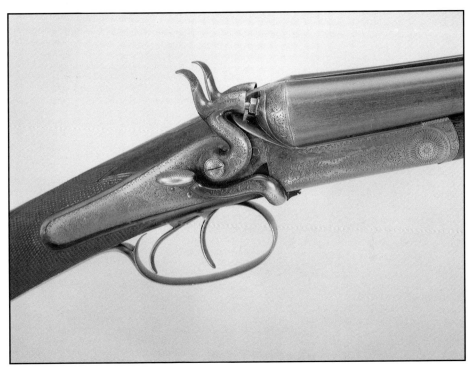

Figure 9 – Round Body Back Action

Boss hammer gun 20-bore; SN 3951; weight 5 pounds, 8 ounces; c. 1888.

This gun is an example of a round body, back action. The main spring is located behind the hammer (tumbler in a hammerless gun). The locks are inletted into the stock with the action uncut.

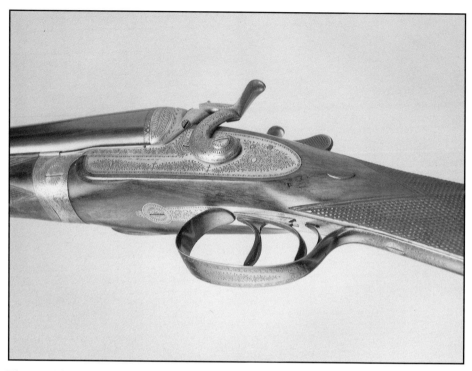

Figure 10 – Wood Bar Action

Wilson hammer gun 12-bore; SN 506; weight 6 pounds, 13 ounces; c. 1880.

This wood bar (or bar-in-wood) action incorporates bar action sidelocks, but they are inletted into the wood that covers the thin action flat (or table). It is a handsome effect.

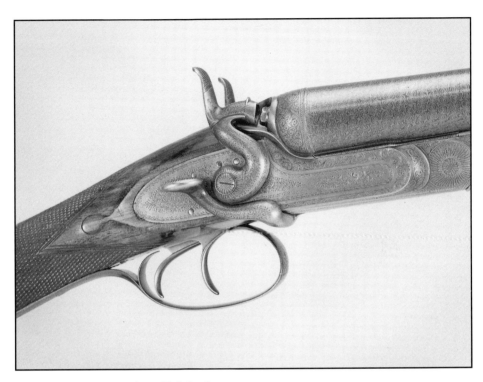

Figure 11 – Bar Action Sidelock

Grant hammer gun 12-bore; SN 5280; weight 6 pounds, 14 ounces; c. 1883.

Pictured here is an example of the bar action sidelock, a rather standard action design. The main spring is forward of the hammer (tumbler in hammerless guns) and mounted on the tongue of the side plate, which is inletted into the action bar.

Some bar action guns have back action locks (main spring behind the tumbler) to increase the strength of the action bar (*see Figure 37*). Also, all over/under sidelocks have back-action locks.

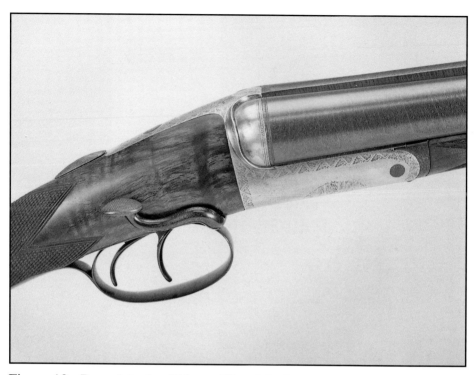

Figure 12 – Round Action Trigger Plate Mechanism

Grant hammerless 12-bore; SN 5105; weight 7 pounds; c. 1883.

This elegant gun is typical of the round action type with a trigger plate mechanism (Phillips Patent of 1879). The tumblers (hammers) are cocked by the sidelever operating mechanism and employ coil springs.

Figure 13 – Concealed Third Fastener

Purdey hammer pigeon gun 12-bore; SN 22100; weight 7 pounds, 5 ounces; c. 1921.

The small projection between and near the top of the barrels (breech end) fits into a slot in the standing breech of the action. A bolt fits on top and holds the barrels down. This late model hammer gun also illustrates short hammer spurs and side clips on the action, which fit matching bevels on the sides of the barrels.

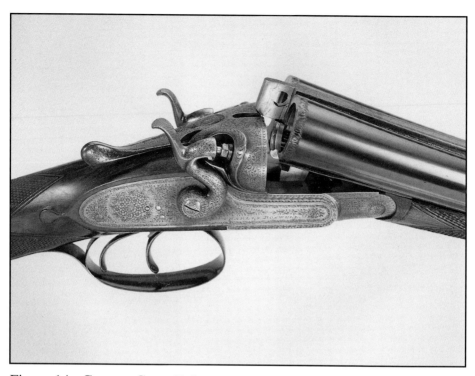

Figure 14 – Greener Cross Bolt

Boswell hammer pigeon gun 12-bore; SN 5612; weight 7 pounds, 13 ounces; c. 1885.

The flat-sided top rib extension with hole, as shown, fits a slot machined into the standing breech. A round, tapered rod engages the hole and forms the third bite, or lock.

The Scott Cross Bolt is very similar, except that it is square.

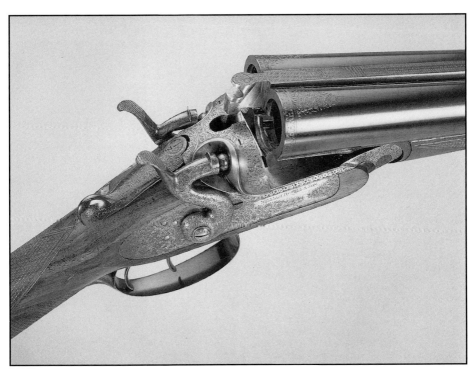

Figure 15 – Doll's Head Fastener

Powell hammer pigeon gun 12-bore; SN 8289; weight 7 pounds, 10 ounces; c. 1886.

The large top rib extension, called a doll's head, fits into the cutout on the standing breech. This example also has the Westley Richards bolt that fits into the notched doll's head. By moving the sturdy, articulated top lever to the side, the doll's head bolt moves rearward to unlock the gun.

Many Westley Richards guns had only this top bolt, but this third fastener is often found in conjunction with underlocking lugs. Also shown here are the engraving panels on the barrels and the typically flat, wide pigeon gun rib.

Figure 16 – Rigby-Bissel Rising Bite

Rigby hammerless 16-bore; SN 15554; weight 7 pounds; c. 1883.

The rising bite patent of Rigby-Bissel is pictured here, which was one of the best and most expensive of the third fasteners. The third bite is unlocked when the rear one-half of the locking wedge moves down, permitting the barrel rib extension loop to move up as the barrels rotate.

This gun also illustrates fluted fences and a dipped edge sidelock. The tumblers (hammers) are cocked by the snap underlever. Two sets of Damascus barrels were made for this gun. Number 1 is a True cylinder X True Cylinder, and Number 2 is 3/4 X Full, both with flat pigeon ribs. An interesting gun.

Figure 17 – Beaded Fences

Lang hammerless 12-bore; SN 13379; weight 6 pounds, 15 ounces; c. 1902

Fences may be defined as the juncture between the flat surfaces of the action body and the rounded hemispheres (balls) of the action that close off the breech end of the barrels. Pictured here are beaded fences.

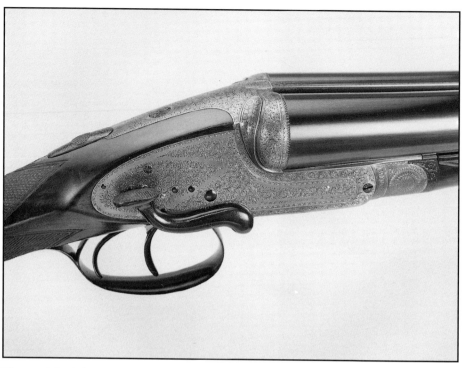

Figure 18 – Fluted Fences

Grant hammerless 12-bore; SN 6647; weight 7 pounds; c. 1894.

This example of fluted fences is typical of Grant guns after 1890. It also demonstrates Grant's extended-width action table (or flat), which offers greater strength.

Figure 19 – Arcaded Fences

Woodward hammerless 12-bore; SN 5445; weight 6 pounds, 10 ounces; c. 1902.

The arcaded fences shown here were typical of the London best Woodward guns. Also illustrated is the extended bearing surface for the tumbler (hammer) axle, which projects slightly from the side plate.

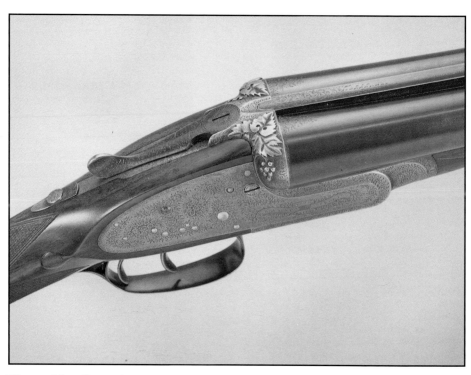

Figure 20 – Carved Fences

Beesley hammerless 12-bore; SN 1238; weight 6 pounds, 12 ounces; c. 1900.
Beautiful, deeply carved fences typical of Beesley guns are illustrated here.

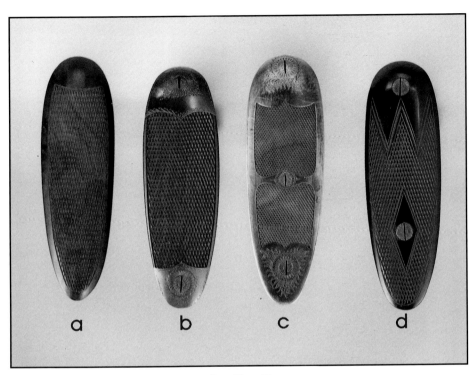

Figure 21 – Types of Treatment for Gun Butts

a. Checkered contoured wood.
b. Steel heel (top) and toe (bottom) plates, with checkered wood interior.
c. Skeleton steel butt plate with checkered wood interior.
d. Contoured and checkered horn, hard rubber, or plastic butt plate.

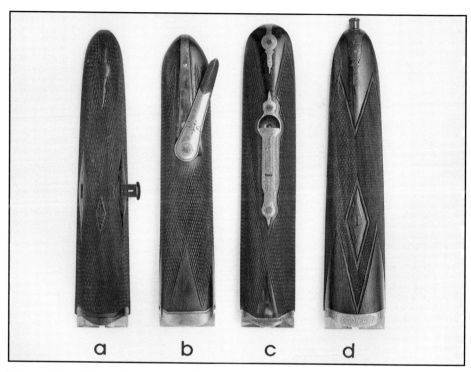

Figure 22 – Normal Types of Fore-end Fasteners

Types a. and b. are inert
  a. Wedge or cross bolt; carried forward from muzzleloading guns and common before 1875.
  b. Lever; very positive; found on many double rifles.

Types c. and d. are spring locks
  c. Deeley and Edge
  d. Anson push rod

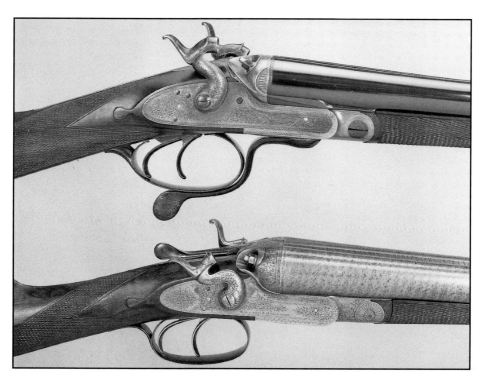

Figure 23 – High Hammers and Low Hammers

Upper: MacNaughton 16-bore; SN 162; weight 6 pounds, 14 ounces; c. 1875.
Lower: Holland & Holland 12-bore; SN 14517; 6 pounds, 11 ounces; c. 1892.

Shown here are two contrasting types of external hammers. Earlier hammer guns had high spurs, which were not so reclined when cocked and were more centrally aligned (therefore closer together). Later guns, such as the Holland, usually had smaller spurs, reclined more when cocked (out of the line of sight), and angled the noses of the hammers inward (resulting in hammers further apart).

The MacNaughton has a Jones rotary underlever. As one of a pair, it was retrofitted with ejectors, an unusual combination. It was recently sleeved as a 32-inch, 20-bore.

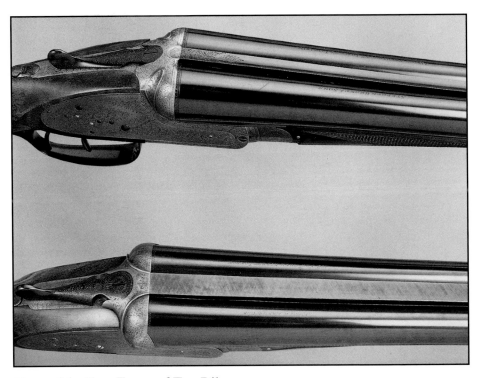

Figure 24 – Two Types of Top Ribs

Upper: Grant hammerless 12-bore; SN 7326; weight 6 pounds, 10 ounces; c. 1903.
Lower: Lang hammerless pigeon gun 12-bore; SN 15731; weight 7 pounds, 12 ounces; c. 1915.

The Grant (above) has a classic game rib with a smooth concave top surface. It is swooped to follow the contours of the barrels. The Lang (below) has a typical pigeon gun rib with a flat top surface. In this instance, it is cut with a file to reduce glare. It is also longitudinally flat from breech to muzzle. All proper ribs should be slightly below the top of the barrels at the muzzle end.

The Grant (above) also illustrates fluted fences. The Lang (below) has beaded fences and side clips.

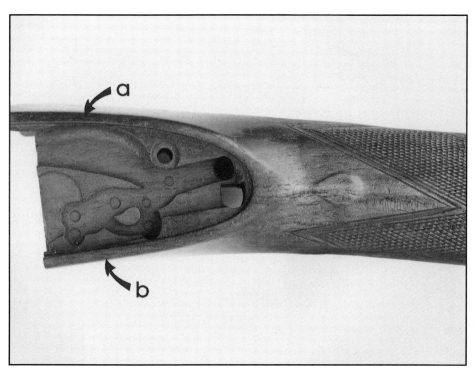

Figure 25 – Inletting

Illustrated in this photograph is the remarkable workability and durability of French walnut. Inletting is a true mirror cast of the inside of the lock, down even to the screw heads. It leaves only an arc at the top for the tumblers (hammers) to fall. Checkering is a further indication of how cleanly the wood works. Points are crisp and sharp, yet do not break off with extended wear. This stock has seen over fifty years of service. The top horn and bottom horn are marked "a" and "b," respectively.

Figures 26a – Action to Wood Fit

These two views (Figures 26a & 26b) dramatically depict the differences between a London best hand inletted stock head and a mass produced, machine inletted, trigger plate over/under stock head. A near perfect fit is critical between the head of the stock and the rear of the action, where recoil stress is transmitted.

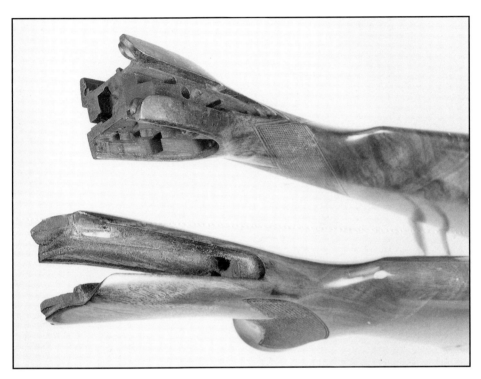

Figure 26b – Action to Wood Fit

The hand crafting is apparent in both views. It demonstrates how the locks, top tang, and trigger plate are perfectly mirrored in the wood and how the stockmaker is able to execute such precise and smooth work-given time, good wood, and proper tools. The machine, inletted stock reflects the results of using high-speed machine tools, which necessitate a design that avoids close fitting in the interest of cost and time of manufacture.

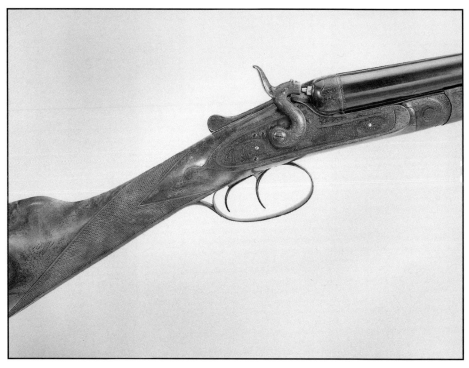

Figure 27 – Straight Grip

Purdey hammer gun 28-bore; SN 10354; weight 4 pounds, 14 ounces; c. 1879.

Purists would argue, with reason, that this straight (or English) grip has the most natural feel and permits the shooter to point the gun more quickly and accurately than any other grip. The sense has been likened to pointing a shaft or spear, with both hands in line, and thrusting forward.

This early hammer gun is also a nice example of long hammer spurs and a wood bar action.

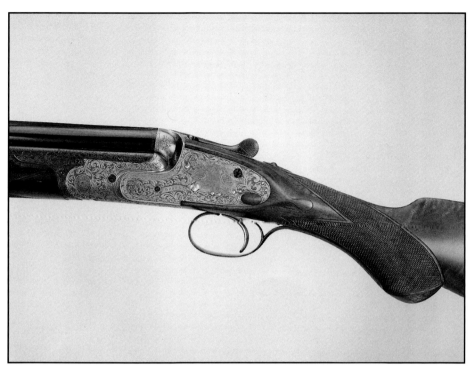

Figure 28 – Semi-Pistol Grip

Boss sidelock over/under 20-bore; SN 8020; weight 6 pounds, 3 ounces; c. 1932

The semi-pistol grip has less curvature (longer radius) than the pistol grip and is therefore intermediate between straight and pistol. It has a feel similar to the straight grip, but it provides a slightly firmer hold on the gun. This grip has always been popular on over/under guns.

Other features of this elegant, well proportioned Boss are its graceful lines, single trigger, and barrel selector on the left lock plate (just above the trigger).

A variation of this grip is the Prince of Wales grip (*see Figure 43*) found on many elegant guns.

Figure 29 – Pistol Grip

Holland & Holland .303 double rifle; SN 17617; weight 9 pounds, 2 ounces; c. 1899.

The pistol grip is favored for guns with heavy recoil because it enables the shooter to maintain a firmer hold. The wrist does not tend to slip back through the right hand. Curvature is greater (smaller radius) than for the semi-pistol grip.

This Holland rifle has back action locks with the main spring behind the tumbler (hammer). The result is a stronger action bar desirable for heavy loads.

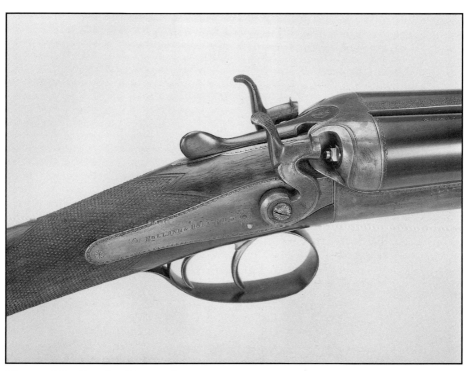

Figure 30 – Border Engraving

Holland & Holland hammer gun 12-bore; SN 15606; weight 7 pounds, 4 ounces; c. 1893. This Paradox gun (rifled chokes) is an example of border engraving.

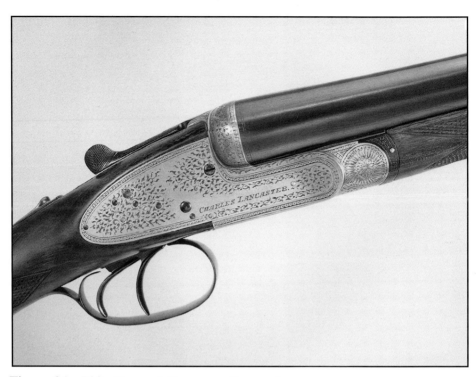

Figure 31 – Fifty Percent Coverage Engraving

Lancaster hammerless 12-bore; SN 12825; weight 6 pounds, 9 ounces; c. 1930.

The engraving time (in man-hours) for this handsome gun is about one-half that required for full coverage. Illustrated here are also triggers that are properly turned for a right-handed shooter.

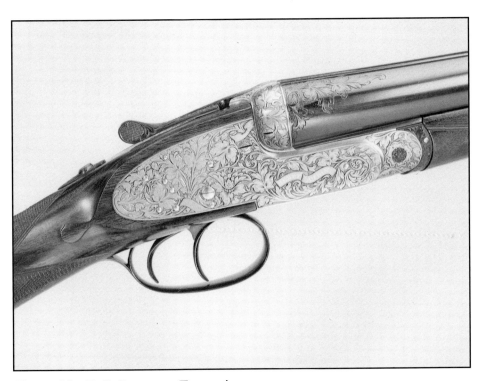

Figure 32 – Full Coverage Engraving

Atkin hammerless 12-bore; SN 24007; weight 6 pounds, 14 ounces; c. 1986.

For full coverage engraving shown here, a bold floral pattern was chosen by the client, who preferred engraving that is easy to see and appreciate. The engraved panels on the barrels are also visible.

Figure 33 – Game Scene Engraving

Grant hammerless 20-bore; SN 24016; weight 6 pounds; c. 1990.

This brilliant example of full coverage, game scene engraving is characteristically English. The work is usually deeper cut than fine Italian game scene engraving, since the guns are expected to see hard service in the field.

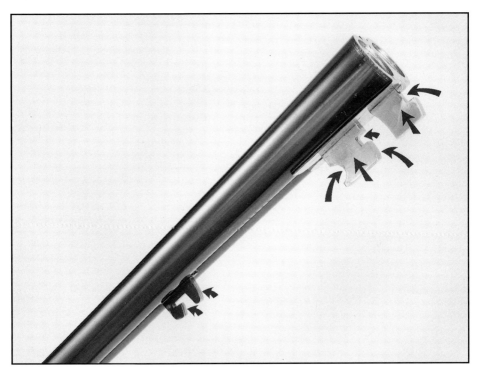

Figure 34 – Points to Lubricate the Barrel Lumps

All of the surfaces designated by arrows in this figure should be lubricated with a drop of high-quality oil or grease each time the gun is taken from its case and assembled for use.

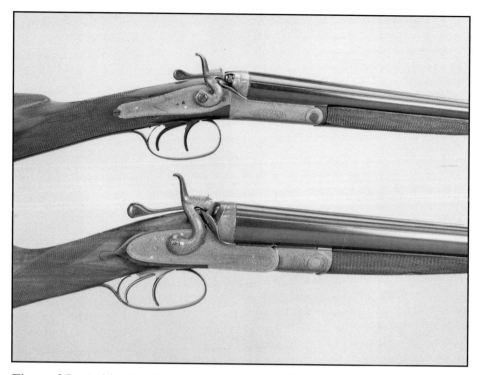

Figure 35 – Achieving Proper Scale at Both Ends of the Spectrum

Upper: Reilly hammer gun .410-bore; SN 23742; weight 3 pounds, 14 ounces; c. 1880.
Lower: W & C Scott hammer gun 12-bore; SN 5684; weight 10 pounds; c. 1880.

When guns are entirely handmade, it is possible to maintain proper scale and balance over wide variation in size and total weight, especially with hammer guns. The extreme comparison here presents a giant that weighs 2½ times its tiny companion. The .410-bore is proofed for ½ ounces of shot, the 12-bore for 1½ ounces. The .410-bore is a round body, back action, and the 12-bore is a bar action gun.

The components of both guns are in proportion, well shaped, and pleasing to the eye. The 12-bore is built to shoot three times the shot weight of the .410-bore, and weighs about three times as much.

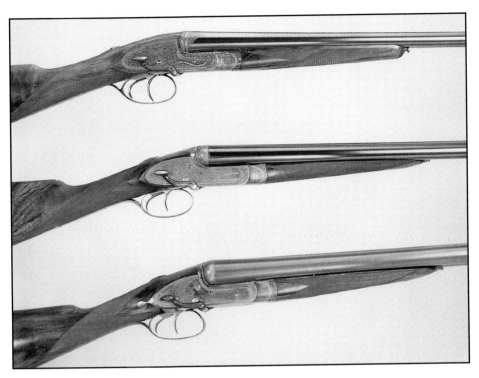

Figure 36 – A Study of Scale

Upper: Grant hammerless 28-bore; SN 24021; weight 5 pounds, 8 ounces; c. 1992.
Middle: Grant hammerless 20-bore; SN 5649; weight 6 pounds, 4 ounces; c. 1886.
Lower: Grant hammerless 12-bore pigeon gun; SN 5621; weight 7 pounds, 6 ounces; c. 1886.

These guns demonstrate several points about scale and how proper proportions and balance are maintained throughout the range of bore size and total weight in hand crafted guns. Of interest is the relationship of barrel diameter to the thickness of the action bar. This ratio remains relatively constant.

Although the wrist (of the stock) is virtually the same for all three guns, the top of the stock at the action (top horns) must be shaped differently on each gun to achieve smooth lines from the barrels back to the wrist.

Fore-ends are essentially the same length, but the 28-bore is slightly thicker to compensate for the lack of width, and thus weight.

The two earlier guns (20-bore and 12-bore) do not show the fluted fences characteristic of Grant guns, from the 1890s forward.

Figure 37 – Scale of Hammer Guns versus Hammerless Guns

Upper: Greener hammer pigeon gun lock; 12-bore
Lower: Holland & Holland hammerless pigeon gun lock; 12-bore.

These two large pigeon guns are comparable, but different in scale. The hammer gun lock is quite noticeably smaller. Even a fine sidelock hammerless gun must be thicker and deeper through the action than a hammer gun to change weight distribution and balance, as well as scale.

The upper lock is a bar action (main spring in front of the hammer). The lower lock is a back action (main spring behind the tumbler, or hammer). Both guns are about the same total weight and each is about seventy-five years old.

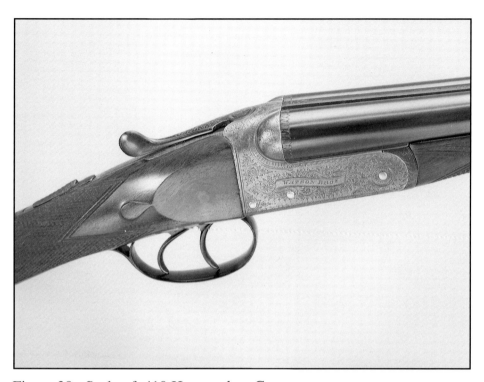

Figure 38 – Scale of .410 Hammerless Guns

Watson hammerless boxlock .410-bore; SN 1908; weight 4 pounds, c. 1920.

It is very difficult to maintain proper scale when fitting .410-bore barrels to a hammerless action. When a well-scaled sidelock .410-bore is attempted, the parts become tiny and are extremely hard to make and fit. Watson Brothers,who specialized in small-bore guns, developed this boxlock as a very close approximation to the proper scale found in .410-bore hammer guns.

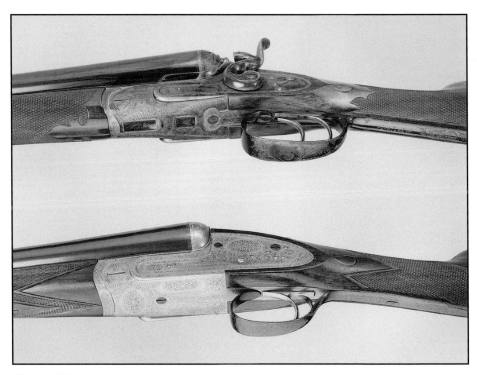

Figure 39 – Lumps Extending through Action

One readily apparent distinction of a London best gun is the fact that the lumps never extend through the action. Illustrated here is a second quality gun (upper) with the lumps showing on the bottom of the action, as compared with a London best gun (lower) with a solid action bar below.

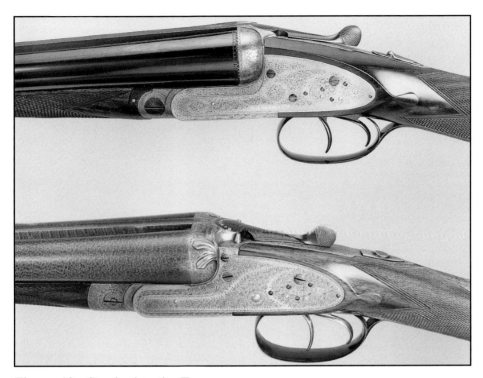

Figure 40 – Stocked to the Fences

In the London best gun (upper), the top portion of the stock (top horns) is continuous to the back of the fences on the action. The other handsome gun (lower) cannot be considered a best gun because it is not stocked to the fences (which in this case are beautifully carved). Certain very early best guns were not stocked to the fences, which constitutes an exception to this rule.

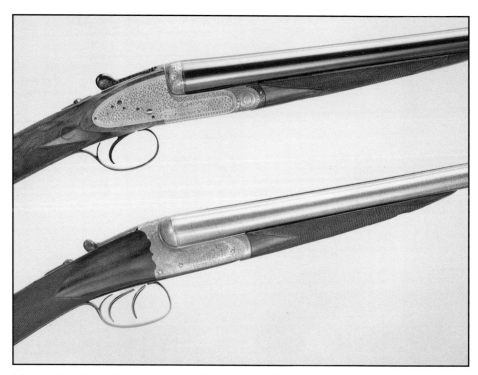

Figure 41 – Sidelock Compared to Boxlock

Upper: Holland & Holland hammerless sidelock;
SN 27866; weight 6 pounds, 12 ounces; c. 1913.

Lower: Westley Richards hammerless boxlock;
SN 15353; weight 6 pounds, 8 ounces; c. 1885.

The upper gun is a best sidelock, with the locks (firing mechanisms) for each barrel mounted inside the flat plates and extending back from the action body on each side. The lower gun, a boxlock, has the locks encased in the hollow action body.

Mechanically, the leverage for the trigger/hammer link is more balanced for the sidelock, which can be seen by the location of the pins that are generally in line between the trigger and the strikers (firing pins). This mechanical balance is not achieved by the more eccentric pin positioning typical of boxlocks.

This Westley Richards boxlock is, however, of good quality. The scalloped back of the action is an indication that it is not a production model.

The shape and size of the trigger guards for the two guns are of interest, demonstrating the basic variation to accommodate double versus single triggers.

Figure 42 – A Rare London Best Gun

Grant over/under 20-bore; SN 24020; weight 6 pounds, 9 ounces; c. 1994.

A current London best over/under with as low a profile as possible and with the proper flow of line from barrels through action and into wrist of stock. Probably less than 800 London best over/under sidelocks have ever been made.

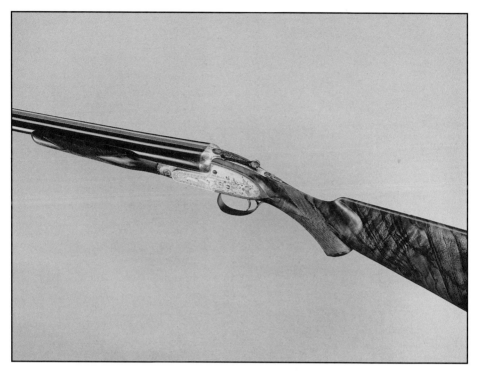

Figure 43 – Best Gun with Nontraditional Features

Atkin hammerless 16-bore; SN 24015; weight 6 pounds, 8 ounces; c. 1990.

Although the client in this instance ordered a gun whose features are more typically American than English (i.e., beaver tail fore-end and single trigger), the grace, style, and proportions have been retained without any loss of appearance or balance.

Figure 44 – Action and Locks in White, Compared to Finished Gun

At the left, an Atkin 12-bore spring-opening action is filed up in the white, with the right lock detached.

The finished gun at the right is also a 12-bore Atkin, SN 3510, c. 1948, that was made to the order of English gunwriter Gough Thomas (Garwood).

Figure 45 – A New Hammer Gun

Grant hammer gun 12-bore; SN 24028; weight 8 pounds; c. 1995.

This recently produced hammer gun was made for helice and live pigeon trapshooting. Even with 34-inch barrels and a 15$^1/_2$ inch stock (pull), the gun balances as specified and is relatively light for its type. Historically, many of the finest guns were made for live pigeon trapshooters.

Part II

Shooting with Consistency

Basics

Important Note: In the interest of text continuity, all references to the left hand, right foot, and so forth are based on the assumption of a right-handed shooter. Apologies are extended to left-handers, who are likely accustomed to reversing references to left and right, a curse of the southpaw syndrome.

Introduction to Part II

The title to Part II was chosen with care. Chapters that follow all place emphasis on consistency, on the basics of shooting with consistency. Most of the millions of Americans who enjoy shooting game birds are plagued with the frustrations of inconsistency. One good shot may be followed by a succession of misses, or one good day may be followed by a nightmarish one.

What are reasons for such inconsistency? Why is it so difficult to replicate successful shots? A flippant, but rather honest answer is: "It ain't as easy as it looks." This is true of most sports, and of most other endeavors for that matter. Professionals make it look effortless, but novices struggle. Years of practice, not native ability, normally account for excellence.

Until quite recently, most American sportsmen began their shooting careers at an early age with little to no formal instruction, except for a few admonitions regarding safety. Hunting is, after all, steeped in the lore and tradition of this nation. A young man was expected to take his trusty shotgun and go in search of game. Hitting flying targets was a skill to be achieved (but often was not attained) by dint of trial and error in the field.

Like much else, the process was and is much more formalized in Great Britain. Here the young sportsman is normally first given instructions at shooting grounds, where basic skills can be more easily and effectively developed. As a result, the Brits are by and large better field shots than those of us from the States. Fortunately, procedural paths seem to be converging today, as more and more Americans recognize the merits of shooting schools.

Beyond getting a correct start is the process of continuing one's shooting education. Consistency is most difficult to achieve without proper investment in the right kind of practice. The exceptional opportunity of sporting clays, now available to the serious shooter, makes practice not only effective, but a pleasant diversion as well (*see Chapter 18*).

Consistency also depends on mastering ingredients of style, and fundamentals that define good style. Individual chapters in Part II are

124

written with the intention of standing alone to some extent, as issues of style and technique are presented. The reader can therefore search for a topic of interest without too much loss of continuity. As a result, however, he may be annoyed by a certain amount of repetition, if he is dedicated to reading in sequence. Repeated elements, however, are usually worth added emphasis.

Virtually omitted from this narrative is a discussion of gun safety, which normally has a rightful place in a "how to" treatise. It was not an oversight. We have such strong personal feelings about safety, courtesy, and manners where guns are involved that a separate book would be required to cover this subject. Shooting with consistency, not gun safety, is the theme here. Nonetheless, there is an obvious overlap, and the importance of safety cannot be overstated.

Though oversimplification is always dangerous, there is one cardinal rule of safety that overshadows all else: "Never point a gun, loaded or not, in an unsafe direction." Most of the hazards one encounters in the field or on the shooting grounds can be avoided if this rule is followed. It is not our intent to diminish the importance of other safety considerations, but none is more fundamental.

The reader is reminded that this entire narrative carries with it an assumption of a right-handed shooter with a master right eye. This convention bears no prejudice toward those who are left-handed. It is assumed that southpaws, having great native intelligence, can reverse left or right references in the proper manner. Admission of political incorrectness is also made, with due apology to fine women shots. He or she additions seem unnecessarily disruptive.

The famous advice of Lord Ripon will be introduced in Chapter 10. It is repeated here: "Hold high and don't check your swing." Good shooting!

✤ Chapter 10 ✤

The Importance of Style

Perhaps the outstanding thing about a good style
is that it makes shooting look easy.
– Gough Thomas

Style and Shooting

Perhaps the most important aspect of achieving shooting consistency is to develop a style that is both sensible and consistent. Shooting style needs to be sensible in the sense that it can eliminate extraneous actions and can focus on those that are important. Consistency in style makes it possible for the shooter to replicate his performance under any conceivable shooting conditions.

The legendary English sportsman Colonel Peter Hawker is supposed to have remarked, "Tis better to miss with style than to hit with bad form." Many Americans find this amusing. Who cares about style if the target is hit? A trip to a gun club will persuade the casual observer that clays can be broken quite easily by shooters with atrocious, even bizarre, styles. What could vindicate Colonel Hawker? The answer is to take the contorted shooters away from their target shooting practice and make them come to terms with a high-curling pheasant or a windblown mourning dove.

The merits of style do bear scrutiny. No one questions Jack Nicklaus's style in his golf swing, nor would the most severe critic take issue with the service motion of Pete Sampras. Sugar Ray Leonard brought his incomparable style to the boxing ring, and Hank Aaron made every hit on the baseball field look easy. It follows that great shooters must also have a style that contains unhurried, fluid movement, a oneness with the gun, and grace that is economical, confident, and consistent.

A stylish shooter has smoothness. He never jumps at the target, never jerks, never stabs. From his first movement to his follow-through the swing is smooth. How is this achieved? It is accomplished in two ways. First, the aspiring shooter must determine what constitutes good style, and then he must, as in any sport, commit himself to thoughtful and dedicated practice to attain his goal.

Like the participants of other sports, a shooter must develop his own style through a personal adaptation of classic or theoretically correct style, as prescribed by such an authority as Percy Stanbury. The shooter's style must fit his physique, his level of coordination and reflexes, and his concept of shooting. Good style does not necessarily mean identical style, but it must be consistent and reasonable.

Fundamentals

A few fundamental precepts help define an effective style. They are advocated by most experienced shooting instructors:

1. Take an open, semifacing, relaxed, and upright stance. Never crouch with exaggerated bent knees (*see Figure 1 for the correct stance and Figure 2 for an incorrect one*). Feet should be a comfortable foot or so apart.

Figure 1. Correct stance

2. Hold the gun high before mounting with the buttstock well above your waist. The muzzle of the gun is normally at eye level and aligned with the expected point of pickup of the line of the target (*see Figure 3*).

3. Keep your weight forward on a straight left leg and the toes of the right foot. A locked, but not rigid left leg becomes the column for level pivoting of the waist as the upper torso unit swings to the left or right.

4. The initial movement of the left hand is critical because it forces the muzzle to follow the target smoothly. Movement of the buttstock to the face and shoulder must come after the initial movement of the left hand.

5. As the muzzle (left hand) moves along the line of the target, the comb of the stock is drawn to the face.simultaneously, the shooter leans into the swing and brings his right shoulder forward to meet the butt. The entire upper torso pivot (swings) from the waist, not just the arms and gun.

Figure 2. Incorrect stance

Figure 3. Point of pickup, (ready position)

6. Ideally, the brain will say shoot at nearly the moment the buttstock arrives at the face and shoulder.

7. The follow-through, like the swing in any sport, is essential. The work is not over when the trigger is pulled. The swing should proceed at the same rate before and after the shot.

In addition to smoothness, good style is characteristically unhurried, or appears so. A key element to this aspect of style is economy of movement, and the left hand. Movement of the gun as it is finally mounted, after first being placed in the ready position, is only a few inches. A target need not be chased if the left hand (muzzle) moves first to the line and draws the buttstock to the face and shoulder.

The three most important means of attaining good style are practice, practice, practice. Each shooter will respond differently when exposed to the basic principles of style, for each individual has a unique concept of what it takes to hit a moving target consistently. Only by repeated effort and thought can an average shooter build on his ability to become a fine shooter. He must think about what he is doing, and he must pull the trigger at countless targets.

Perhaps the greatest of all field shots was Lord Ripon, whose advice was repeatedly sought by his contemporaries from all levels of shooting ability. His laconic response was simply, "Hold high and don't check your swing." Obviously, this style concept "meant it all" to him.

✤ Chapter 11 ✤

Gun Mounting – A Key Element

The mounting of the gun is a deliberate, smooth and comparatively slow movement and the body is relaxed until the instant of firing.

– Percy Stanbury

Proper mounting of the gun may seem to be quite rudimentary and a subject that scarcely justifies detailed consideration. An experienced shooter might be inclined to move on to more pressing and complex matters. Most instructors would agree, however, that good execution of this basic step is actually rather sophisticated and involves several peripheral issues, such as stance, hand and foot positions, a mounting process, gun fit, and individual physique variations. Consistent mounting has everything to do with consistent shooting.

Stance

A good starting point is proper stance and how the target is addressed. Although it may be argued that there are no absolutes in the matter of stance, the following works well for most good field shooters:

1. The target (more properly its line of flight) is addressed almost by facing it, as opposed to a position that aligns the hips parallel

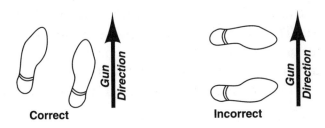

to the gun barrels (*see Figure 1 for the correct position and Figure 2 for an incorrect one*).

2. The left leg is straight with a locked but not rigid left knee.

3. Weight is forward on the left leg and toes of the right foot (right heel slightly off the ground). The shooter is definitely not flatfooted and will incline forward slightly as the left hand moves to the target (*see Step 4 below*).

4. During the process of actual mounting, the shoulder moves forward to meet the butt, as the head moves forward slightly to press into the comb of the stock.

5. Posture is upright but relaxed with the head forward and vertical, not inclined.

The open stance described above may seem awkward to anyone accustomed to a closed stance, but it clearly offers a wider range of mobility, particularly when swinging to the left. The locked left leg provides a stable column and makes it easier to keep the swing level. Rotation is from the waist. The shoulders should remain basically level for most, but not all, types of shots.

It is important to remember on passing shots that the target should be addressed (and the open stance oriented) at the point where the target is to be taken, not toward the point where it originates.

Mounting Process

Actual mounting of the gun may be thought of as a two-step process, although it need not proceed in two distinct phases. Arriving at the ready position from an at-rest condition is the first step in the sequence. The end product of this step is an alignment that places eye, tip of the muzzle (front bead), and line of flight of the target in the same plane, with the buttstock between the biceps and ribs and slightly (two to six inches) below the pocket where it will ultimately fit (*see Figure 3*). The pocket is that location on the shoulder between the collarbone and the ball of the arm and shoulder joint.

Many shooters seem obsessed with a starting position at the waist (*see Figure 8a*). Mounting the gun from this remote destination is not desirable for several reasons. A long trip to the shoulder creates unnecessary haste, encourages a tendency to rotate the gun about the left hand like a baton, and makes consistent mounting much more difficult. In a word, it is not economical. Since smoothness in developing the line of the target is synonymous with economy of motion, a ready position that minimizes travel is definitely preferable.

The second step in mounting the gun should always begin with movement of the left hand, which extends along the line of flight of the target. The left hand also has the secondary function of drawing the stock forward from under the right arm. Lifting and setting the stock's comb into the face by the right hand is almost an unconscious result of the lead role of the left hand. Naturally, the butt of the stock is, in the same sequence, moving into the shoulder pocket. However, the shooter should concentrate on drawing the comb to his face. The butt will find the shoulder as he leans into the swing.

Ideally, the mounting process is completed at almost the same time as the brain orders the finger to pull the trigger. This culmination of events virtually ensures that the shooter will not track the target or lift his head off the stock, which are two of the most common technical shooting flaws.

Consistency

Consistent mounting is critical to successful results, for it permits the shooter to concentrate solely on the target. He knows the gun is in the proper alignment and position (assuming a correct gun fit). He may also rest assured that effects of recoil will be minimized if the gun is mounted correctly.

In this latter regard, recoil should never be a concern if certain straightforward conditions are met. First, a reasonable cartridge load must be employed for the weight of the gun being used. Second, the gun must be correctly fitted for the shooter. Third, the gun must be firmly (but not rigidly) held, so that recoil can be absorbed by the entire body. There is no reason for a black-and-blue shoulder or biceps, no matter how many rounds are fired, if these conditions are met.

Unfortunately, consistent mounting is not automatic for the average shooter. It requires thoughtful and repeated practice. A serious mistake is the usual form of practice in which the shooter simply lifts the gun to his shoulder repetitiously. This activity encourages initial movement of the right hand and consequently builds the wrong muscle memory.

Instead, mounting practice should always incorporate the correct sequence. Start from the ready position, then move the left hand first and establish a line, while drawing the gun forward and out from under the arm. A very good routine is to face the corner of a room with the gun held high in the ready position and with the eye and front bead aligned with the point where walls and ceiling converge. Move the left hand first along the line of the ceiling and one wall and draw the comb of the stock to the face (and the butt out from under the arm and to the shoulder). Do this twenty times to the left and twenty times to the right. Use snap caps and dry fire at the instant the buttstock settles into the pocket. This practice really works. It will also reduce muscle fatigue under live conditions.

Another tip for consistent mounting is to elevate the right elbow somewhere between forty-five degrees and a horizontal position (*see Figure 4*). This position helps create the pocket. Check on consistency

Figure 4. Right elbow up to create pocket, index finger of left hand extended along barrel.

by closing your eyes for several repetitions, and then open them and confirm that your master eye is centered on the rib.

The correct and comfortable position of the left hand on the fore-end (or barrels) may vary somewhat from shooter to shooter, but generally speaking the left arm should be slightly less than fully

Figure 5. Thumb/index finger position

extended. It is important to point the index finger of the left hand along the barrels as an aid to guiding direction along the flight line of the target (*see Figure 4*). On side-by-side guns, this position of the index finger has the added advantage of keeping other fingers from the top of the barrels.

Exact placement of the trigger finger is perhaps arbitrary, but a good case can be made for positioning the trigger between the tip of the finger and the first joint, an obvious advantage for double trigger guns. Likewise, the position of the right thumb is debatable, but a firmer grip seems to be achieved by extending the thumb across the wrist of the stock (*see Figure 5*).

Figure 6. Correct fit

Figure 7. Incorrect fit

Gun Fit (*see Shotgun Fit in Chapter 19*)

It is critically important that the gun adequately fits the shooter (i.e., proper drop, length of pull, and cast off). The gun will then easily and naturally come to the eye when mounted correctly. By no means should the head ever be lowered to align with the sighting plane (*see Figure 6 for the correct fit and Figure 7 for an incorrect one*).

Unfortunately, most American guns come off the shelf with no cast off and a standard amount of drop (usually 2½ inches). The shooter therefore finds himself adapting to the gun by tilting his head to align his eye with the barrels. This slight contortion creates serious inconsistency. Moreover, the head should be held vertical to see the target better and to ensure a level swing along the line.

It is difficult to compensate for improper drop and cast off (*see Chapter 19*), but if length of pull (from trigger to the center of the stock butt plate) is not ideal, considerable adjustment can be accomplished by positioning the left hand on the fore-end or barrels (further extended if the gun is too short and placed in more closely if too long).

It is hard to overstate the importance of practice in mounting, yet few shooters will invest the necessary time. Only by countless repetitions can muscle memory and consistency be attained. When correct mounting finally becomes an unconscious certainty, the shooter can then concentrate totally on the target.

✤ Chapter 12 ✤

Lead and the Left Hand

The left hand does the real aiming.

– Robert Churchill

Lead Theories

Most writing on shotgunning deals heavily with the critical matter of lead, or swinging through. This emphasis is understandable. Most beginning shooters are astonished to discover that a passing target at thirty yards distance actually requires so much forward allowance. Indeed, it is the bane of instructors that this seemingly apparent principle is so difficult for some novices to grasp, much less to believe.

In shooting literature, endless arguments are advanced to support the rationale of the swing through method on the one hand, or the virtues of sustained lead on the other. If one is patient enough to winnow through various theories and supporting narrative, he will probably come to the conclusion that each of the different schools of thought has reasonable merit, and that the issue of lead is largely in the eye of the beholder.

Absence of a single, overriding approach is not surprising. The variety of circumstances that affect lead, such as distance, speed, angle, direction, height, and wind, all militate against a single answer to the question of where to shoot in order to hit a given passing target. Physics of the matter may be definitive, even calculable, but the application of theory is subjective to say the least.

Role of the Left Hand

Our intention is to wipe the slate clean and depart somewhat from traditional schools of thought. We may accept each as correct, but consider each somewhat relative. Any approach to the matter of lead must recognize two circumstances. First, each individual sees a target differently, and secondly, the targets themselves offer a perplexing variety of lead requirements. The conceptual approach advocated is simple and is straightforward. The real secret is the left hand.

Consider the case of a passing shot with obvious lead requirements. What are the response reactions of an average shooter?

1. One way or another, he reads the shot. His visual software program goes into action.

2. More likely than not, he mounts the gun, that is, the right hand moves the buttstock to his face and shoulder.

3. He chases after the target, in most cases with great haste.

4. He establishes lead, either by swinging through, or by a conscious determination, the sustained lead technique.

5. Bang, he shoots, at which point he may or may not stop his gun.

This sequence (*see Figures 8a, 8b and 8c*) can produce successful results, depending on the experience of the shooter. It is evident, however, that a target pursued in this manner can be missed in four ways: above, below, in front, or behind.

Figure 8a. Gun too low for start

Figure 8b. The quick mount

Figure 8c. Chasing target after mounting

142

Consider now a more effective response that is keyed to the left hand (*see Figures 9a, 9b and 9c*).

1. The shooter reads the speed and direction of the target by focusing on its line of flight.

2. The gun is positioned so that his eye, the inclined tip of the muzzle, and the line of flight of the target are in the same plane (*see Figure 9a*).

3. He moves and extends the left hand along the line of the target to overtake it. This step is often called developing the line (*see Figure 9b*).

4. At almost the same moment of overtaking the target, the comb of the stock arrives at his face, drawn there by the left hand, and only unconsciously lifted by the right. In the process, the shooter had leaned forward so that his shoulder rolled into the butt (*see Figure 9c*).

5. Almost simultaneously, he instinctively establishes lead, pulls the trigger, and follows through with no change in the rate of swing.

Figure 9a. Correct ready position

Figure 9b. Left hand moves to line

Figure 9c. Gun fits into cheek

If steps 4 and 5 are virtually simultaneous and if step 3 is accurately negotiated, then the success ratio is high for two compelling reasons. Two of the four ways to miss have almost been eliminated–above and below. There was no opportunity to track the target or to pick up the head, two common shooting flaws.

It is hard to overstate the importance of the left hand. It must move first and extend along the target's line of flight. The gun must be drawn through the target and into the mounted position. Follow through must be executed in a continuous movement.

In the second, more effective sequence described above, the most difficult execution problem is likely to be step 3, evenly following along the flight line of the target. Two concepts seem to help. First is to imagine that the left hand, with index finger extended, is merely pointing along the line. This concept can be demonstrated without a gun by pointing along the line of a target with the left hand, palm up and index finger extended.

A second concept, advocated by some instructors, is for the shooter to imagine that the target has a vapor trail extending along behind it. He is then encouraged to follow up the vapor trail until he passes the target. Both of these concepts are useful, but effectiveness will frankly depend on the mind-set of the individual.

Unfortunately, none of the recommended approaches can assist a novice shooter with exactly how much lead is required for a given shot because lead depends on a unique combination of the many variables cited above. The real teacher must be experience. One categorical observation, which is based on experience, is that swinging through alone will not get the job done on fast passing targets at near maximum legitimate range. These extreme cases require substantial visible lead. Let no one persuade you to the contrary.

When a shooter, novice or not, consistently misses a given long passing shot behind, which is the usual case, it is the practice of many instructors to insist that he double the lead, as the shooter sees it. More often than not, this advice must be repeated twice, even three times. When at last the shooter breaks such a target, he is normally astonished. Other instructors use the technique of challenging the shooter to miss in front. Even with this rather harsh harassment, long passing shots are seldom missed because of too much forward allowance.

Lead is also a very real thing in the field, where birds are at considerable range. A helpful hint on these types of shots is to focus on a spot well in front of the bird. Almost all shooting authorities would agree that at least 85 percent of unsuccessful, long-passing shots are missed low and behind.

How, then, can the dominant left hand help resolve this problem? A part of the answer is aggressiveness. Shots requiring substantial lead require a different mind-set. These targets must not be approached timidly. The left hand must not only be dominant, but assertive, powerful, and authoritative. Such aggressiveness need not, and should not, be at the expense of smoothness. It is the combination that produces results, in addition to lots of practice.

High-passing shots add a slightly different dimension. There is the obvious matter of adequate lead, plus a tendency to fall off the target at just the point of firing. Shooting instructors are almost universal in urging the shooter to extend more with the left hand, which helps him maintain the line rather than falling off the target as the swing progresses. Many shooters have a marked tendency to droop the shoulder, particularly the right shoulder on left-to-right shots, which can also be overcome by deliberate extension of the left hand (*see Figures 10a, 10b, and 10c*).

Figure 10a. Line of high right-to-left target

Figure 10b. Incorrect; weight shifts to right leg

Figure 10c. Correct; weight remains on left leg

The Barrel Plane Concept

Closely related to the essential role of the left hand and the importance of developing the flight line of the target is a concept that is described as the barrel plane concept. It is often quite helpful to shooters.

First, consider a double-barrel gun and imagine a horizontal plane passing through the two barrels, as illustrated by the black cardboard in Figure 11a. Next visualize a high-passing shot where the target is rising, say a pintail after the alarm of a first shot. To aid in establishing the flight line, think in terms of a slight rotation of the barrels and your shoulders so the imaginary plane coincides with the flight line and slices along it as the left hand extends and guides the muzzle through the target (*see Figures 11a, 11b, 11c, and 11d*).

Figure 11a. Picking up the target

Figure 11b. Rotating barrels and shoulders, gun still not mounted

Figure 11c. Following along line of target as the gun mount proceeds

Figure 11d. Slicing through line and final mount

Most birds in the field do not proceed horizontally, especially from point of view of the earthbound shooter. This concept of rotating the barrels and aligning the imaginary plane along the line of flight makes one particularly conscious of a rising bird and prevents missing from below, which is a common error.

Of course, the imaginary plane is perpendicular to a vertical line through the barrels of an over/under shotgun, but the thought process of the plane following along the flight line remains the same.

✤ Chapter 13 ✤
Footwork Is Fundamental

A good shot starts from your feet.

– Ken Davies

Footwork

Both footwork and foot position are essential to consistent shooting, but these subjects receive little attention. Basic principles of footwork and foot position are often overlooked or underrated, which is a serious oversight. In nearly all other sports, especially those involving a ball, the importance of footwork is clearly recognized. It is even taken for granted. Yet, it is seldom given proper emphasis by shooters, who are absorbed instead with issues of hand-eye coordination, lead, and follow through. Footwork, though, is almost as fundamental in shooting as in other sports.

Some appraisal of field experiences are in order. Consider a quail that inexplicably flushes back to your side instead of flying away from you. Most shooters react by twisting in a spiral knot and try unsuccessfully to catch up with the bird. Where were the feet? Probably dug in like columns, steady to wing and shot. Hitting such an unexpected shot is made remarkably easier by simply moving the feet, turning, and taking the bird straight away.

What about a high-incoming dove or pheasant that is missed on the first shot as it passes over. Again, the normal reaction is to attempt a second shot past the zenith in a most awkward arched-back posture that virtually ensures a miss. The alternative is to make a smart 180-degree, about-face, followed by remounting the gun with the muzzle high, and smoothly dropping down through and below the departing bird, a proper lead in this instance, somewhat like High Station One on the skeet range.

This same principle applies to many opportunities for doubles. A slight repositioning of the feet before the second bird is picked up makes all the difference. An extreme example, of course, is an incoming pair or flight with one in front and one behind.

Most shooters unconsciously feel there is inadequate time for footwork adjustments, but this notion is simply not valid. The best place for experimentation is obviously at shooting grounds under controlled conditions with clay targets. Novice and experienced shots alike are invariably surprised to discover there is ample time to move the feet and that favorable results are dramatic.

Even in the marsh or duck blind there is usually time to shift the feet in such a manner as to take strain and awkwardness out of a tough shot. It is quite possible, of course, to shoot sitting down (some few do it well), but a really smooth swing clearly depends upon its foundation.

Foot Position

Another aspect of consistency has to do with foot position, as opposed to footwork. Foot position in this context has to do with the placement of the feet once a shooter has correctly shifted his body to roughly face the flight line of the target.

Most beginning shooters feel more natural at the outset facing sideways to the target (line of flight) with the long axis of the gun parallel and close to the plane of the shoulders and chest. The genesis of this stance no doubt derives from one or two reasons. It appears to be more comfortable because the center of gravity of the gun is closer to the body and makes it seem lighter. Another reason comes from previous experience firing a heavy rifle (*see Figures 1 and 2*).

Lessons of field experience, however, prove a definite advantage of the open stance (*Figure 1*), where the shooter more nearly faces the target. This stance provides greater mobility of swing to right or left, with obvious improvement in addressing the awkward bird to the left. It also facilitates consistent mounting that places the butt squarely in the pocket. In this secure position, recoil can easily be absorbed instead of causing the butt to slip out and bruise the biceps or face.

Without a doubt, footwork and foot position are both fundamental parts of consistent performance.

✤ Chapter 14 ✤
Who Says Both Eyes Open?

He had but one eye, and the popular prejudice runs in favor of two.

– Charles Dickens

Background

Somewhere in the dark recesses of American shooting lore there arose the maxim of both eyes open. Although most people fired a rifle with the left eye shut, youngsters were told to keep both eyes open when it came to shooting a shotgun. Origin of this myth was no doubt founded on the premise of better visibility, of seeing and judging a target better. Well enough, but this valid point does not tell the entire story, which is rather complex.

Any shooting instructor will tell you that individuals vary enormously in the way they see targets, variances that go far beyond actual acuity of vision. Determining how and what the shooter "sees" is, in fact, one of the most difficult challenges in teaching. Consider the fact that the great hitters of baseball can even see the ball making contact with the bat. Some could allegedly see the ball compress on impact. The legendary masters of service return in tennis have eyes that judge a ball traveling at 125 miles an hour and can make near perfect contact. At the other end of the eyesight spectrum, some individuals totally lack the ability to measure the speed, direction, and distance of a moving target.

Eye Dominance – the Master Eye

Dominance, or lack of dominance, of a master eye further complicates the vision issue in shotgunning. Most people have a master eye to some extent. This phenomenon may be loosely defined as the eye that controls where the shooter is actually looking at the time the trigger is pulled.

The master eye (or more rarely, a lack thereof) can be determined by looking at a distant object through a reasonable size peephole at arm's length. After focusing on the distant object with both eyes open, a person should then close first one eye and then the other, holding the peephole steadfastly in place. The object will remain in view for the master eye, but will vanish for the other for most people. If the object vanishes for both eyes, no strong master eye is indicated, and the individual is said to have central vision, which is unusual.

Normally (but not without considerable exception), the right eye dominates for right-handers and the left eye for left-handers. Reversals are common. Can you believe that eye dominance is not the same in men and women? Some authorities state positively that only ten percent of men, but ninety percent of women, are left-eye dominant. There is no question that women incline toward left-eye dominance, even if one does not accept the ninety percent assertion. There are other variables. Eye dominance does not even remain constant for some shooters throughout the course of the day or for two different kinds of shots, one angling from the left and the other from the right. Many knowledgeable shooters maintain that such elements as fatigue affects eye dominance.

Shooting instructors, who deal with all of these vision irregularities on a regular basis, normally recommend that a person shoulder his gun on the same side as his master eye, regardless of whether the individual is in other instances right-handed or left-handed. This is good advice, since it is really not difficult to adapt to this change, but it is impossible to change one's master eye. Oddly, most people strongly resist this recommendation, particularly if they have had any past shooting experience–regardless of whether this experience has been successful or not.

Thesis

All these considerations lead to the conclusion that is the general thesis of this chapter. Both eyes should not, for many individuals, be open at the time the trigger is pulled, regardless of eye dominance.

It is time now for qualifications. No one would question the universally recommended practice of focusing both eyes on the line of flight of the target. Only at the moment when the left hand moves through the target and draws the comb of the stock to the face and the butt to the shoulder should the left eye be closed, or at least be winked.

More qualifications involve fortunate individuals who do not experience difficulty with both eyes open and can ignore the thesis. In these cases, however, it is worthwhile to establish if this circumstance is valid for all types of shots. Some other individuals cannot close one eye in the recommended way for one reason or another. It is advisable then to block out the left eye by partially obstructing its view in some manner, such as transparent tape of the left lens of the person's shooting glasses.

In all cases, the shooter should do some serious practice to resolve the best means of accommodating problems related to eye dominance. It is time well spent at the shooting grounds to try many passing shots with both eyes open and many with the left eye closed at the time of firing. Similarly, both techniques should be tried on trap targets.

Even though individuals vary greatly, many shooters will discover that both eyes open is not the right medicine at the moment of pulling the trigger.

✤ Chapter 15 ✤

Instinct versus Tracking

The ideal condition would be, I admit, that men should be right by instinct ...

— Sophocles

The vast difference between the rifle and shotgun can be well illustrated by comparing the mechanics taking place during the trigger pull. One is deliberate, reasoned, and steady, while the other is a flash of instinct.

It is difficult for novice and experienced shooters alike to place confidence in instinct, to know the right instant to pull the trigger. Most sports that involve hand-eye coordination do not offer much in the way of last-second timing options. The ball must be struck at a precise moment. A shotgun target, however, presents timing choices, which is something of a mixed blessing. On the one hand having choice offers more opportunities for success, but on the other hand, it introduces the perplexing variable of when to shoot.

The right time to pull the trigger almost defies logic in view of individual differences in response time, vision, and other intangibles. Targets also vary infinitely. It is probably fair to say that no two people would shoot the same difficult target at precisely the same moment, yet each may be shooting at a proper time for himself.

Some light, however, can be shed on the matter of timing. The shooter who moves smoothly to the target with his left hand and mounts his gun as he swings through it should shoot at the first instinctive moment his brain suggests.

There is really no time for thinking. On shooting grounds, thinking should be done before a shot is taken. In the field, it is best left in the car during the heat of the action. There is no real justification for tracking a target or trying to consciously measure lead. Once the instinctive moment has passed, the odds of hitting the target are exponentially reduced. He who hesitates is lost.

A few more words about tracking are in order. This counterproductive tendency to stay with a target too long has haunted nearly all shooters at one time or another. It is particularly evident in the field and in competitive events where the stakes for hitting are increased. Consider the following sequence of events:

Things are going well for a shooter. He has just nailed three birds in a row. Now he misses an unusually tough, twisting bird, and the miss puts a slight dent in his confidence. On his next try, a tiny bit of caution creeps into his brain, instructing him to rely less on instinct and be just a little more deliberate. Now he is in trouble. His hesitation causes him to miss this bird and the next one. A progression of caution unfolds. At this point, the shooter needs to give himself a good talking to, and he must return to placing full confidence in his instinct.

For the so-called natural shot, reliance on instinct may come quite easily. For those who must acquire shooting skills through a great deal of effort, it must often be forced; however, neither the natural shot nor the hesitant one is immune to backsliding into tracking. Both must constantly remind themselves that the time to pull the trigger is the first available instant the target is "right," preferably at almost the same time the comb of the stock comes to the face.

A shooter must trust his instinct. More often than not, it is correct.

✤ Chapter 16 ✤

Three Shooting Flaws

It is always interesting to ask experienced shooters and shooting instructors what they consider to be the three most common shooting flaws. While they can usually agree that most people miss low and behind on passing shots, there is often less consensus on the primary reasons for missing. Once the beginner has learned to mount the gun properly, and once he has overcome the usual problems associated with lead, what are the most common causes for missing? Why do competent shooters miss targets they would normally hit? The answer obviously has much to do with shooting well consistently.

All authorities would not agree, of course, but a strong case can be made for the following three problems: (1) tracking; (2) picking the head up off the gun; and (3) stopping the swing. Each is surely a cardinal sin, yet each can be corrected with a little concentrated effort and thought. Each can be a product of habit, or each can be a sometime thing.

Tracking, the characteristic of staying with the target too long, is the most insidious flaw, because the more you miss, the more you are inclined to track. It is a vicious cycle of cause and effect. Once the slightest cloud of doubt erodes confidence in pure instinct, the shooter loses that split-second best time to pull the trigger. Tracking is then inevitable and nearly always causes a miss.

Proof may be found in examples. Almost no quail shots are missed as a result of tracking. It all happens so fast, or seems to, that the shooter relies unconsciously upon instinct. Waterfowl, driven pheasant, and long passing shots at a clay target are other matters. There may be too much time, which causes the shooter either to measure off or to track. Too much thinking in this case is a bad thing.

Closely aligned to tracking is the flaw of lifting the head off the gun at the last moment. This unfortunate error ruins the nice theory that you shoot where you are looking, true only if the gun is properly and steadfastly mounted. Picking up the head usually results from taking too much time, although it can occasionally be a form of flinching, or recoil anticipation. In the latter case, the gun, if it is well fitted, should simply be held more firmly. In the former case, it is a matter of improved timing.

Both tracking and lifting the head can be cured by moving the left hand along the line of the target before bringing the comb of the stock to the face. As the muzzle passes through the target and the gun is actually mounted, trigger pull should be virtually simultaneous, an instinctive reaction. If this sequence is properly executed, it is almost impossible to track or to pick up the head, which is a little easier said than done. Practice is the answer.

The third shooting flaw is a nemesis to everyone at one time or another. In the beginning, new shooters tend to stop the gun when they pull the trigger or when their brain says to pull the trigger. Bang and stop, which is usually stop and bang, if the truth were known. It is a habit which, if ingrained, is extremely difficult to overcome.

Stopping the gun is also an erratic flaw of experienced shooters, particularly those individuals who are characterized as natural shots. The shooter-athlete relies so much on his native instincts, which carry him ninety percent of the time, that he overlooks follow-through. Other competent shots have the disguised flaw of stopping only on right-to-left, or left-to-right, shots. This tendency is not apparent to the shooter, who must usually be told by an instructor, or an experienced friend, that he is stopping his gun.

Another common cause of sporadic stopping comes from looking at the barrels. If a shooter shifts his focus from the target to the barrels, he will usually stop swinging because the target vanishes.

The shotgun itself has a major influence on follow-through. Short barrels are favored by a surprising number of shooters, most of whom do not realize an abbreviated barrel length contributes to stopping the swing. A muzzle-heavy gun swings slower, but more evenly than a muzzle light gun. A butt heavy gun may seem lively and fast, but it is more difficult to control and much easier to stop. The better solution is a longer, barreled gun balanced about the hinge pin.

Almost all sports require follow-through and shooting is no exception. Before and after pulling the trigger, swing must be continuous and smooth with neither acceleration nor deceleration. An easy way to prevent stopping the swing is repetitious exaggeration on passing clay targets. By repeatedly swinging through, perhaps more than is really necessary, and by not stopping when the trigger is pulled, muscle memory ultimately eliminates the need to *think* about not stopping. It is a very difficult habit to correct in the field, when your mind is on so many other things.

Fortunately, recognition is ninety percent of the battle in overcoming these three flaws. A little concentrated practice can work wonders.

✥ Chapter 17 ✥

An Extension of Basics

General

This chapter examines some of the special situations that are likely to be encountered in shotgunning. In most instances, these types of shots can be replicated on shooting grounds with clays, where a serious shooter can refine his skills to accommodate the situations he will meet in the field. In other cases, however, he will only confront the circumstances in the field. A few tips based on experience may prove helpful.

Some Special Shots

1. **High Incomer.** When a high incoming target is approaching dead on with no passing component, it is difficult to develop the line, swing smoothly through the target, and pull the trigger without a slight drift to the left. This phenomenon results from two causes. First, the target or bird is blocked from sight by the barrels as the swing-through takes place. Second, the moving unit of torso, arms, and mounted gun simply drifts naturally to the left for most right-handers.

   This tendency can be easily demonstrated. Stand directly under a high beam and face down its longitudinal axis. Try to swing precisely along the beam through the apex of the swing and note the tendency to drift to the left. The remedy is to shoot slightly to the right of the target or at the left wing. The results are surprising. Incidentally, the need for and amount of this correction is even more pronounced with most American guns, which ordinarily have no castoff to alleviate the problem (*see Chapter 19*).

One other point should be made about high incomers. As the target approaches its zenith over the shooter, weight of the body should still be on the left leg. A shooter may find himself running out of swing and in danger of slowing or stopping his wing. This problem can best be overcome by arching the back, not by a weight shift (*see Figure 12*). Practice is essential.

Figure 12.   Correct form at apex

2. **Long Passing Shots.** Another curious phenomenon has to do with the amount of lead on longer passing shots from left to right, as compared with right to left. Logic would tell us that for any given distance and speed, forward allowance should be the same. This is not so in practice. The right-hander requires more apparent lead from left to right. The longer the distance, the more the difference. The reason is the rate of swing. A shooter pushes the left hand and turns the upper body on shots from left to right, as opposed to pulling with the left hand on shots from right to left. The angular velocity (rate of swing) of the pull is simply faster than that produced by the push.

Since it is difficult, if not impossible, to adjust for this slight difference in rate of swing, the answer to the discrepancy is in the amount of apparent lead. On close-passing shots, this effect is not so significant, but on long-passing shots, the apparent lead on left to right targets can be twice that of the same right to left target, depending somewhat on each individual's sight picture. It is definitely a matter that should be determined on shooting grounds under controlled conditions.

Another point of caution on left to right targets is that there is a marked tendency to shift the weight from the left foot to the right one. This inclination should be resisted, because it interferes with an even rate of swing and it encourages the right shoulder to droop, which pulls the muzzle down from the line of the target. Remember that the left hand requires more extension on this shot (*see Figures 10a, 10b, and 10c*).

3. **Very Low Incomers.** Very low incoming birds present yet another optical problem. Although this shot is relatively rare for most Americans, it is a common with driven grouse shot in Britain. On rare occasions, however, duck hunters confront low incomers. While the shooter "covers up" a normal incomer, very low-flying birds must be treated quite differently or the shooter will shoot over the target. A good concept to overcome this tendency is to think how the bird would look if it were dangling its feet, and shoot at the feet. The results will then be dead-on.

4. **Selecting the First Bird to Shoot.** Whether it be coveys, flights, or simply two passing birds, it is always a rather confusing split-second decision to choose which single target to take first. Obviously, there is no pat answer, but a few suggestions are worth considering.

First of all, there is usually more time than most shooters think is available. A conscious, determined effort to take an extra look before swinging into action pays handsome rewards. Certainly, it is a mistake to mount the gun too soon. Remember that movement of the left hand is the first order of business.

Secondly, don't always take the obvious bird, the one that first catches your eye. This obvious target often makes your second shot, for the double, more difficult, not to mention that your shooting partner will invariably choose the same bird. Think of the eye-catching quail in a covey rise, the one that comes back or separates from the pack. Why him? Why not two or more birds closely positioned?

Consider the case of two passing birds at equal range. Which should be shot first, the lead bird or the one following? Take the following bird first so that swing is uninterrupted for the second shot and a logical double. Notice, too, that this sequence will cause less reaction (alarm) to the second (lead) bird. In spite of being patently reasonable, this correct choice is seldom made.

Consider the situation when you have two birds dead away, one slightly lower. Which one do you shoot first? The lower one, so the first shot does not obscure the sight picture for the second, especially when you consider the effects of recoil. The same principle applies to covey rises. Start at the bottom and work up. It keeps the birds in view.

In all cases for doubles, there is a cardinal rule. "Focus only on the first bird." If this bird is well hit, it is then time to move to the second. If the first bird is missed or poorly hit, stay with it for a second shot. This advice is fundamental, because it is based on a tendency that seems ingrained in human nature. If full concentration is not given exclusively to the first bird, a shooter is strongly inclined to let his eye wander to the second target and usually causes him to shoot somewhere between the two. If his thought process is to shoot twice at the first target, he is far less apt to make such a mistake.

An even more technical consideration is what to do about two high incomers dead-on. Which one should be shot first, the left or right? The answer is the left bird for right-handers, because the gun may tend to slip out of the pocket to the left after the first shot. If the right target is taken first, there is a strong tendency to miss to the left on the second, left-hand bird. If, however, the left target is taken first, then it is necessary to reestablish from scratch the line of the right-hand target to better assure a hit. Remember, shoot slightly to the right on both.

5. **Remounting between Doubles.** The next bit of advice may test your credibility. It is often advantageous to remount between doubles. Curiously, most shooters see better and rely more confidently upon instinct and muscle memory when the process of picking up the line, mounting, and swinging-through takes place for each shot.

   This suggestion does not apply, however, for two birds dead away or to a second shot following a miss by the first. It is valid for most opportunities for passing doubles, but requires conscious effort and practice.

6. **The *Almost* Incomer.** Finally, there is the case of a high, thin-angle incoming bird. By thin angle is meant less than fifteen degrees, if dead-on is zero degrees and a full passing shot is ninety degrees. It is very difficult for most shooters to develop the line on this flight pattern, compared to the dead-on target. There is a tendency to intercept or to drift off the line with a thin-angle incoming bird. A helpful solution for some is to change the foot position slightly, rotate the shoulders, and develop the line as a high passing shot.

   This technique may seem awkward at first and definitely requires practice, but it permits the shooter to see lead and maintain line. Critical to its success is a good starting look at the target, movement of the feet and a slight rotation of the hips and torso, and good extension of the left hand (*see Figures 13a, 13b, and 13c*).

   Incidentally, it may be necessary, as for all very high targets, to place the left hand on the fore-end slightly less extended than for the normal passing shot to avoid binding at the apex of the swing. If the left hand can not swing freely,

Figure 13a. Picking up the target

Figure 13b. Repositioning of feet

Figure 13c. Weight on left leg

the muzzle will drag off the line to the left and inscribe an arc instead of a line.

It is certainly advisable to practice this technique on shooting grounds and to compare it with the normal method of taking high incomers. Under these controlled conditions, each individual can determine what is best for himself. Universal appeal is not claimed, but many shooters find the technique quite helpful.

7. **Focus on the Target.** Once the shooter has determined that a shot is safe, it is critically important that he focus his vision and his attention solely on the target. It is not sufficient and not productive to focus in the area of the target. With intense concentration, focus at some forward portion of the target or at a point in front of the target for long-passing shots. Under no conditions should the shooter ever look at the

gun barrel or focus on the sights, which will in all likelihood result in a miss.

Tips from the Field

1. Learn the importance of range and how to estimate it. In reality seventy percent of all game birds are killed within twenty to twenty-five yards, ninety percent or more within thirty to thirty-five yards. In spite of allegations to the contrary, no one consistently kills birds at fifty or more yards, even though those who claim this ability may cripple birds at this range. Effectiveness and sportsmanship alike suggest a forty-yard maximum range.

    It is a good practice in the beginning to measure off actual distances on the ground from a given reference point, in order to refine one's ability to estimate range. Most new shooters are surprised at how far a forty-yard target looks from their standing perspective.

2. It is particularly difficult to estimate range on high overhead shots. When it is thirty-five yards up, even a bird as large as a pheasant looks hopelessly out of range. The illusion is enhanced when the target is, for example, a white-wing dove. Shooters must be more aggressive on these shots, but remember, all the while, that a high, long-passing shot is probably just as far as it looks.

3. A good tip has to do with a quick second shot at a bird not well hit. If a quail still has his head up, you had better hit him again to avoid losing a wounded bird. This practice is particularly applicable to ducks and other larger game birds. A second shot is simply a good rule if the bird is not "dead in the air." The shooter may lose some opportunities for doubles, but one clean kill would seem to have merit over one or possibly two difficult retrieves. It is, moreover, easier to hit a wounded bird in the air than on the ground or water, not to mention safer in most cases.

4. Shooting through trees or brushy cover is a curious matter that comes with field experience. It might seem logical to avoid such shots, under the assumption that the pattern would be wrecked by any such obstruction. Oddly enough, the reverse is usually true. Generally, if the shooter can still see the bird through interference, the shot charge will do its job.

    Some shooting grounds are laid out to prove this point. It is always amazing that clay targets can be broken consistently if the shooter will just concentrate on the target and ignore the leafy obstructions.

5. Marginal light at dawn or evening duck-flighting in Great Britain presents another optical anomaly that suggests a deviation from normal practices of lead. Generally, these birds are closer than one judges them to be, thus less lead is required. It is worth trying to concentrate only on the head or a few inches in front of it.

These suggestions are extensions to the basics presented earlier and should be addressed only after mastering the fundamentals.Refinements such as these, however, do seem to increase confidence, improve consistency, and provide an incremental "edge" for the experienced shot. It is time well spent to listen to the tips of successful veterans. Their concepts may not always translate to another shooter, but it is certainly gratifying when they do.

❖ Chapter 18 ❖

Sporting Clays

Clay pigeon shooting provides good practice, providing you understand its limitations when applied to game shooting. Competitive clay shooting, for its own sake, is a specialist subject and the technique is different from that required for live birds.

– Percy Stanbury

Origin

In the United States, sporting clay shooting grounds were simply not a part of the world of shotgun sports until the late 1970s and early 1980s. In spite of its late arrival, acceptance has been rapid and widespread. Its antecedents, however, have deep roots in Great Britain, as do so many other aspects of shotgunning.

Sporting clay fields were an outgrowth of shooting grounds originally maintained by prominent gunmakers. The first reference in gun literature is about facilities established by Joseph Lang around 1827, using live birds. Other specific dates of origin are a bit fuzzy, but Sir Ralph Payne-Gallwey mentions practice at Holland & Holland's Kensal Green shooting grounds in 1896. It is likely that West London (a shooting school) and the Boss shooting grounds dated from this turn of the century era, or perhaps before.

By the 1920s sporting-clay fields were relatively common in Britain. Today, there are probably no less than 300 such shooting grounds, but some are only open for competition. After World War II, Americans began participating in driven bird shoots in Britain to a much greater extent. In due course, they learned this demanding sport required skills that could be honed by the exceptional instructors at shooting schools, notably those of Holland & Holland and West London.

It was then only a matter of time until popularity of sporting clays in the United Kingdom crossed the Atlantic. By the early 1990s, there were perhaps 700 or so sporting-clay fields in the United States, though most only operate off and on, and many are not public facilities.

Traditional Clays versus Sporting Clays

Although traditional skeet and trap have been standards of the American shooting scene for many, many years, there has always been minor controversy about the merits of these games for developing skills needed to shoot birds in the field. While there may be some controversy over its value, an objective observer realizes that there is much to be learned from any clay targets and from practice in general.

The routine of most competitive skeet and trap shooters to employ a mounted gun with clays is perhaps most criticized as a failing by field shooters. It should occur to critics, however, that nothing prevents one from shooting skeet or trap with an unmounted gun as good preparation for the field.

Sporting clays, on the other hand, cut through objections to clay targets as a means of improving field shooting. Clever utilization of towers and concealed traps make it possible to project targets from almost any conceivable direction, angle, height, and speed. The principal objective of sporting clays is to simulate the flight of game birds, and this can be accomplished quite well.

Impact on Shooting with Consistency

It is a recurring theme of this book that one must practice, practice, practice. The type of practice is most important, however. In the field, it is quite difficult to correct shooting faults or to refine techniques for hitting complex shots. Seldom do wild birds present the same shot twice in a row, not to mention many other diversions that take place in the field. There are certain lessons that can only be learned from birds in the field, but the shooter owes it to himself to perfect basic skills with clay targets.

Sporting clays offer the best means to become a competent field shot, whether it is a beginner or a veteran who wants to improve his field sport. Not only are these shooting grounds an opportunity to master rudiments, but a place where the most challenging targets can be presented and solved. It goes without saying, a qualified instructor is a virtual *must,* certainly in the beginning. Such instruction has long been a tradition in Britain, but has only recently been recognized fully in America. Fortunately, a growing number of certified teachers of the art are available in the United States, several of whom have benefited directly from the tutelage of Ken Davies, the Rose brothers, David Olive, and other fine English instructors.

Unlike skeet or trap, where scores become an objective, sporting clays should be approached as a learning experience. A good shooter will profit by passing lightly over what he hits well and seeking out his own particular weaknesses. He can then work diligently to come to terms with those targets he finds most difficult.

Unfortunately, there is a safety concern on some public fields that limit the shooter to fixed-position cages. This restriction is driven by the concern for liability but it hampers the advantage to be gained by moving freely to points where target angle or distance presents the most realistic line of flight or the greatest challenge. It does not, however, completely destroy the net benefit. The restriction falls more under the heading of a frustration, although probably an unnecessary one.

Sporting Clay Competitions

Given the nature of the human animal, it is understandable that sporting clays would evolve into competitions. No criticism is intended of these events, which have merit in themselves to participants. It is worth observing, however, that they provide little benefit as a means of improving field skills.

Those who are responsible for laying out competition courses in their zeal to foil expert shooters often resort to targets that resemble nothing one would likely encounter from birds in the field. Moreover, timing distortions necessary to score well in competition can be inimical to field shooting.

This observation is not to say that great competition sporting clay shooters are not splendid field shots. They are, but it is to the distinct advantage of most shooters to improve their skills by carefully considered practice on realistic shots and not on competition targets.

✣ Chapter 19 ✣

A Primer on the Tools of Shooting with Consistency

For fools rush in where angels fear to tread.

– Alexander Pope

Qualification and *Disclaimer*

Opinions vary widely on the subject of how shotguns and cartridges influence shooting with consistency. Any shooting instructor will probably agree that individual gun and cartridge preferences are so ingrained in a person's mind that it will influence his performance, whether from psychological or real reasons.

It has been shown time and again that a shooter will perform noticeably better with one gun than another, even if the two are quite similar in type, weight, and apparent dimensions. A serious shooter must, therefore, try numerous guns and cartridge combinations to determine what is best for his physique, personality, and sense of gun balance.

This presentation is offered with an admitted bias. It must be clear from reading Part I, "The English Shotgun," that the tool of choice is a double-barrel gun, preferably an English side-by-side double. The preferred double has external hammers, double triggers, and no ejectors. After all, it is reliably reputed that God shoots a Grant sidelever hammer gun with thirty-inch Damascus barrels made around 1890.

No apology is made for this acknowledged prejudice. It is, moreover, based on honest comparisons of nearly every conceivable type of shotgun, made over a period of about ninety years. If the reader fails to agree with the weapon of choice, a likely circumstance, he may, nonetheless, find certain observations illuminating.

The Shotgun

There are valid reasons beyond prejudice why double-barrel guns perform so well in the field: balance, dependability, choice of choke, and safety. Although the perfectly acceptable over/under shotgun has obvious appeal to thousands of shooters, particularly their low price, a purist would likely give the nod to the side-by-side double. Consider the following arguments concerning the gun of choice for the field:

1. Side-by-side doubles have the ultimate to offer in weight, balance, and liveliness.

2. Ease of opening and loading the side-by-side cannot be matched.

3. Double triggers are much more logical and effective, because two triggers permit instant choice of choke between the right and left barrel.

4. Double triggers are also much, much simpler mechanisms, hence they are considerably more dependable.

5. Straight grips permits the incremental and unconscious movement of the right hand associated with two triggers. They also tend to point more quickly and more naturally.

6. Ejectors versus extractors are a matter of preference. All else being equal, the simpler the gun, the better. Extractors arepreferable where it is important to leave no cartridges on the ground.

Just as controversial as the matter of shotgun type are issues of chokes, barrel length, bores (gauges), point of balance, and weight. There is obviously no one answer for all individuals, nor for all types of game being shot. Wide variations of opinion alone would suggest that dogma is not justified. The observations that follow have a *general* basis in fact and experience.

Choke: For *most* shooters in *most* circumstances, a strong argument can be presented for ¼ (improved cylinder) choke in the right barrel and ½ (modified) choke in the left barrel. For special purposes, a case can perhaps be made for ¾ (improved modified) choke and full choke, but there is questionable technical merit for an extreme full choke pattern, not to mention the skill required to hit consistently with it.

A good, general purpose choke combination for the double trigger gun is ¼ and ¾, which provides a wide range of choice, say from twelve to forty yards. There would appear to be little logic for two ¼ chokes, but this combination seems quite popular for driven birds and most competitive sporting clay shooting.

Barrel Length: From a purely technical standpoint, there is no evidence of length advantage after about fifteen inches. Shot velocity of any given modern cartridge is about the same whether the barrels are sixteen inches or thirty-four inches in length. From a shooting standpoint, however, most qualified experts will agree that very short barrels start moving and stop swinging (or check) too easily. Longer barrels are smoother to swing, easier to point accurately, and are less inclined to check. On full size guns to be used by persons of normal height, barrels of twenty-eight inches in length should be the minimum. The upper limit is normally thirty-two inches. From an overall balance point of view, barrels should be about twice the length of pull.

The following quote from a great shot, Sir Ralph Payne-Gallwey, written a hundred years ago, is of interest:

> A sportsman who has been in the habit of using a gun with the long, swinging, easy balance given by a thirty-inch barrel, will at once notice, when aiming, the stumpy, unhandy, ill-balanced, tumble about feel of a gun with barrels of several inches less, though the gun itself may weigh lighter in the scale.

It is less well understood that the speed at which a shooter swings a gun has little to do with barrel length and everything to do with the overall shotgun balance. A muzzle heavy gun is slow and a butt heavy gun is fast, regardless of barrel length. Thus a muzzle heavy gun with twenty-five-inch barrels is not as lively as a gun with thirty-inch barrels balanced on the hinge pin.

For the type of shooting that regularly calls for long passing targets, a slightly forward point of balance is advantageous. For reflex shooting in heavy cover and for quail that requires quick pointing, a lighter gun balanced at the hinge pin is more effective for most shooters.

Rib configurations and sights are almost totally subjective matters that virtually defy scientific analysis. What a shooter has found to be best suited to his liking is exactly what he should use.

Bore: Choice of bore (gauge) has become somewhat of an obfuscated issue over the years, particularly in America. There seems to be a notion that better shots use smaller bores, with the ultimate achievement level being the .410. This unfortunate precept has little merit if it is examined in the light of shotgun ballistics, cartridge loading, and common sense.

While it is a pleasant and acceptable diversion to enjoy a 20-bore or 28-bore with light cartridge loads for doves and quail, it is questionable to use them for larger birds, such as waterfowl and pheasant. The .410-bore has no real place in the field even though a legion of devotees, who admit to no wounded birds or foreshortened range, may be angry at this statement.

Ballistically, the 12-bore excels, having with normal loads, the best ratio of shot charge depth to bore diameter, and hence the shortest consistent shot string. This ratio is also quite good for the 28-bore, incidentally. Pattern sizes relate more to choke than to bore, but density is naturally superior for the 12-bore, which usually has more pellets.

It is, moreover, fallacious to think solely in terms of bore diameter. The wide selection of cartridge loadings available today present the shooter with a dizzying set of options. A lightly loaded 12-gauge cartridge may actually have fewer pellets than the heavier 20-gauge shells. So what's macho now? Is it the 20-bore with heavy loads, or the 12-bore with light loads?

There is absolutely no quarrel here with 20-bores or with 28-bores for the proper game bird, but neither should anyone look askance at 12-bores for any type of use. Choice of bore has no relationship to the skill level of the shooter.

It is interesting from a historical perspective to review relative numbers of 12-bore guns versus other bores. Greener wrote in 1910 that for every 10,000 12-bores, there were twenty 16-bores and one 20-bore. This extraordinary ratio probably held true until shortly after World War II, at least in Britain. In recent years, smaller bores have become increasingly popular in the United States, but 12-bores still outnumber all other bores by large multiples. Needless to say, vintage 20-bore or 28-bore English guns are rare.

Weight: Weight issues can be argued endlessly without much light being shed on the subject. One observation is rather undeniable, though. Americans seem to prefer heavier game guns than their British counterparts. This opposing preference probably derives from the fact that machine-made American guns are almost always heavier than handmade English guns. In addition, the type of shooting normally encountered is different. Lighter English game guns seem to function well for driven birds, while the heavier guns balanced forward are quite effective on the long-passing shots so common in American field shooting.

Individual preference seems to be the case for quail, with proponents advocating the qualities of both lighter and heavier guns. Most authorities would agree that 12-bore game guns should weigh between 6½ and 7 pounds. There does emerge consensus on both sides of the Atlantic that competition pigeon guns should be heavier, in the order of 7¼ to 7¾ pounds. As in the case of barrel length, the point of balance probably has more to do with feel than actual weight. No one answer seems to fit every situation.

Shotgun Fit: Shotgun fit stems essentially from stock dimensions and configuration. Most American guns come off the shelf with 14 inches of pull, 2½ inches of drop at the heel, and no castoff (*see sketches for definition of terms*).

For an average, medium-build shooter, say 5 feet, 10 inches in height, a 14 pull is probably only about ¼-inch too short, which can be accommodated fairly easily by slightly extending the left hand on the fore-end or barrels. Taller individuals require greater pull. A reasonable guide is as follows:

Height	Pull
6 feet	14¼ to 14¾ inches
6 feet, 2 inches	14¾ to 15¼ inches
6 feet, 4 inches	15¼ to 16 inches

Variations depend somewhat on the thickness of the chest and on arm length. There is, by the way, no logical basis for the traditional test of confirming proper pull by cradling the buttstock in the crook of the elbow and testing whether the trigger finger can reach the trigger comfortably. This procedure is simply not valid.

Pitch is a term that relates to the angle of the buttplate. It may be defined as the deviation (angle) of the muzzle from the vertical, when the butt of the gun rests on a horizontal surface. From a practical standpoint, however, pitch determines how the buttstock fits the shoulder of the shooter, as illustrated above. A correct pitch ensures that the butt makes even contact.

Pitch of the buttstock is largely a matter of shoulder shape. It can be a significant fit problem for some individuals, affecting as it does

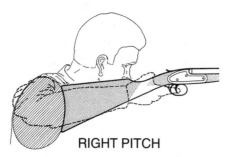

RIGHT PITCH

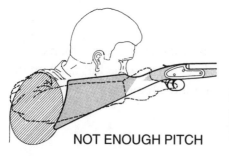

NOT ENOUGH PITCH

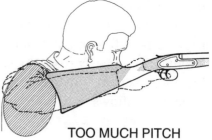

TOO MUCH PITCH

how recoil is transmitted to the shooter's body and face. (*See the sketches on the preceding page that demonstrate correct versus incorrect pitch.*)

More commonly encountered are problems associated with drop and castoff (cast-on for left-handers). Most shooters tend to miss below in the field, which reinforces a strong argument for a drop measurement of from 1½ to 2 inches, which is less than the standard drop of 2½ inches. Whatever the actual measurement of drop, the point of impact (center of the pattern) should be slightly high, say four to eight inches above the point of aim. This feature of shotgun performance is individually discrete and can only be verified positively on the pattern board.

Since it corrects a tendency to miss to the left, castoff is also quite important, especially on high-incoming targets and going-away targets after a hurried mount. For average facial structure and positioning of the eyes, ¹/₈-inch castoff at the heel and ³/₈ inch at the toe is normal. Some shooters with wide faces, though, need as much as ½ inch and others with angular faces and wide set eyes may require none.

Women have a marked tendency to place the comb less firmly into the cheek and almost invariably perform better with more castoff than men. It is also of interest that the less drop a gun has, the more castoff it requires.

Changing drop and/or castoff for most guns can be accomplished rather easily by bending the stock at the wrist, using one of several techniques performed by specialists who know wood characteristics well. Although the owner of a fine gun might have reservations about possible damage, a reputable mechanic of this art has few failures, and total rebound is relatively rare.

Issues of fit are brought into proper focus by consideration of the ultimate objective: a gun that can be mounted repeatedly and rapidly in precisely the same position with respect to the eye and point of aim. Achievement of this goal eliminates the need for alignment adjustments and permits the shooter to concentrate on the target and develop the line. It also enables him to bring the gun to his face, not his face to the gun, an important aspect of the successful mount (*see Chapter 11*).

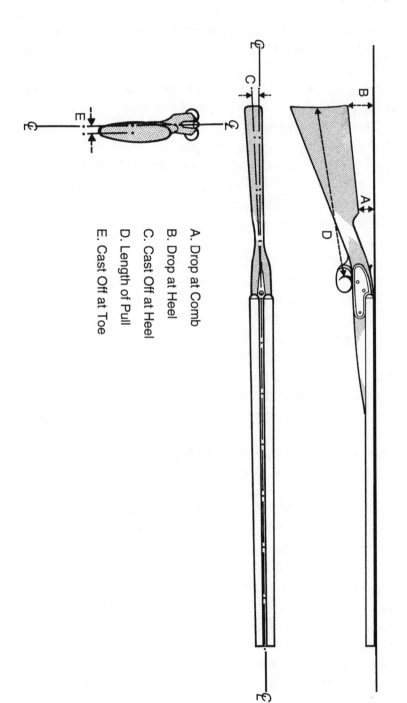

STOCK DIMENSIONS

A. Drop at Comb
B. Drop at Heel
C. Cast Off at Heel
D. Length of Pull
E. Cast Off at Toe

Another way of stating the matter is that when a gun fits the shooter properly, he has no need to look at the gun under any circumstances. A shotgun is not to be aimed.

Cartridge Data

Since there is virtually a limitless amount of ballistic data and claims regarding different cartridge loadings, pellet sizes and composition, powder types, wad design, and myriad other considerations, no attempt will be made to cover even a portion of the available information.

Instead, only a few interesting points bearing rather directly on shooting with consistency will be offered. First, game birds should, by and large, be taken with the smallest size shot that will effectively do the job. Secondly, the high-velocity, heavier loads are not at all what they are reputed to be for normal field shooting.

The first point is difficult to prove, but is based on collective experience of many knowledgeable field shooters. The statistical rationale is that four smaller pellets result in less wounded birds than one larger pellet. Common sense must dictate, however. One would not use Number 8 shot for geese.

The second assertion is positive sacrilege to those advocates of "lots of brass" and probably to cartridge manufacturers who prefer the profit margin on heavier loads. There is ample evidence, however, that high brass loads produce more blown patterns and flat pellets, aggravate recoil, are sometimes destructive to lighter guns, and do not put more birds in the bag than lighter loads.

It is a rather consistent claim of those who champion high-velocity shells that less forward allowance or lead is required. The chart on page 136 relates to Eley cartridges, but would vary only in minor detail from a like comparison of American loads. The preamble to the published chart is quoted as follows:

Velocities and Forward Allowance

Eley standard game loads have a nominal velocity of 1,070 ft/sec. Eley high velocity loads have a nominal velocity of 1,120 ft/sec (at 15 yards).

One might suppose that the change in velocity would make a noticeable difference to the forward allowance, but, as will be seen from the table, the question is one of inches in a forward allowance measured in feet. The difference may, for all practical purposes, be ignored. The comparison chart is as follows:

COMPARISON OF CARTRIDGES Birds Crossing at 40 m.p.h., English No. 6 Shot		
Range	30 yards	40 yards
Forward Allowance Standard Velocity	5 feet, 6 inches	8 feet
Forward Allowance High Velocity	5 feet, 3 inches	7 feet, 8 inches
Difference in Lead	3 inches	4 inches

This chart reveals that even at the maximum reasonable range of 40 yards, the eight-foot lead for a 40-mile-per-hour crossing target is only four inches less with a high velocity cartridge. No more need be said.

Another interesting subject has to do with shooting under windy conditions. High winds can sometimes be ignored, but a strong crossing wind does affect the shot string. Consider the following table of actual test results:

Range (yards)	Wind Velocity (m.p.h.)	Shot Deflection (inches)		
		No. 6 Shot	No. 7½ Shot	No. 9 Shot
40	10	6	7	8
	20	12	14	16

These data reveal that at a range of 40 yards and a crossing wind velocity of 20 miles per hour, Number 9 shot will be blown (deflected) 16 inches, (which is a more serious lead consideration than standard versus high-velocity cartridges).

Ordinarily, it is better to ignore wind and rely on instinct. There is a notable exception, nonetheless. On a long-passing shot at a bird plowing dead into the wind, one must not reduce the lead (forward allowance) to accommodate for the apparent slow speed of the bird, for the shot would be blown behind. This bird should be treated as if it were proceeding at its normal speed, unless it is very close.

Most shooters have strong opinions with respect to favored shot sizes, based on personal experience. Few of these preferences, however, seem to originate from an appraisal of pellet count (and therefore pattern density) for different loadings. As a result, the following chart may be of interest:

NOMINAL PELLET COUNT						
U.S. Shot	Weight of Shot Load (in Ounces)					
Size	$^1/_2$	$^3/_4$	$^7/_8$	1	$1^1/_8$	$1^1/_4$
9	292	439	512	585	658	731
8	205	308	359	410	462	512
$7^1/_2$ 175	263	306	350	394	438	--
6	113	169	197	225	254	281

One final bit of statistical information that is useful for those who shoot outside the United States has to do with shot size equivalents. Unfortunately, there is no universal standard that establishes a precise definition, with the result that slight variations occur from country to country. The table that follows compares American shot size designations with comparable equivalents in Britain, France, Italy, and Spain.

NOMINAL SHOT SIZE EQUIVALENTS					
Metric (mm)	American	British	Italian	Spanish	French
2.8	6	5	5	6	6
2.6	-	6	6	-	-
2.4	7.5	7	7.5	7	7
2.3	8	7.5	8	7.5	7.5
2.2	-	8	-	8	8
2.0	9	9	9.5	9	9

It is well to become acquainted with the look of various shot sizes. When shooting in other countries, the surest means of shot size confirmation is to open a shell and actually examine the pellet diameter.

Selected Annotated Bibliography

Part I – The English Shotgun

Selected Annotated Bibliography
Part I — The English Shotgun

Abbiatico, Mario. *Modern Firearm Engravings*. Rome: Edizioni Artistiche Italiane, 1980. English text; great photographs of Italian engraving.

Akehurst, Richard. *Sporting Guns*. New York: G.P. Putnam's & Sons, 1968. Sixteenth through nineteenth-century guns and shooting; well illustrated with photographs and drawings.

————. *Game Guns and Rifles*. London: G. Bell & Sons, Ltd., 1969. Excellent coverage of nineteenth-century English guns and rifles.

Angier, R.H. *Firearms Blueing and Browning*. Plantersville, South Carolina: Small Arms Technical Pub. Co., 1936. A treatise on how guns are "blued."

Arthur, Robert. *The Shotgun Stock*. New York: A.S. Barnes & Co., 1971. Good basic information.

Austyn, Christopher. *Modern Sporting Guns*. London: Sportsman's Press, 1994. Well prepared with excellent photographs.

Bailey and Nie, E. *English Gun Makers*. London: Arms and Armour Press, 1978. List of early Birmingham and provincial gunmakers.

Baker, D.J. *Royal Guns at Sandringham*. London: Phaidon-Christie's Ltd., 1989. Marvelous photographs.

Beaumont, Richard. *Purdey's*. Oxford, England: David & Charles, 1984. A history of the Purdey company.

Black, D.H.L. *The Mantons, Gun Makers*. London: Historical Firearms, 1993. A history of the Manton brothers.

Boddington, Craig. *Safari Rifles*. Long Beach, CA: Safari Press, 1990. Good, basic information on double rifles and cartridges.

Boothroyd, Geoffrey. *The Shotgun: History and Development*. Long Beach, CA: Safari Press, 1993. The Boothroyd books in this list are essentially a compilation of magazine articles taken from *The Shooting Times*.

————. *Shotguns and Gunsmiths*. Long Beach, CA: Safari Press, 1994.

————. *Sidelocks and Boxlocks*. Amity, Oregon: Sand Lake Press, 1991.

————. *Boothroyd on British Shotguns*. Amity, Oregon: Sand Lake Press, 1993.

Boughan, Rolla. *Shotgun Ballistics for Hunters*. New York: A. S. Barnes & Co., 1965. Basic shotgun ballistics explained simply.

Burrard, Major Sir Gerald. *The Modern Shotgun*. New York: A. S. Barnes & Co., 1931 (reprints). Volume I – *The Gun* and Volume II – *The Cartridge*. Rather technical but contains valuable information.

———. *Guns and Shooting*. New York: A. S. Barnes & Co., 1947 (reprint). Less technical but very informative.

Coxe, Wallace. *Smokeless Shotgun Powders*. Wilmington, Delaware: E. I. DuPont de Nemours Co., 1933. A mine of information on powders.

Crudgington, I. M. and Baker, D. J. *The British Shotgun*. Southampton, England: Ashford, Buchan & Enright, 1979. Volume I–1850-1870. Volume II–1871-1890. Probably the best technical books on the mechanics of double guns. Volume III is promised in the future.

Eley Cartridge Company. *Eley Diary*. London, England: Eley Cartridge Company, 1995. Printed annually; useful gun and cartridge information.

Fiofconi, Cesar, and Guferio, Jordan. *The Perfect Gun*. London: Sotheby Parke Burnet, 1718 (reprint). Translated from the original Portuguese; a good text on early gunmaking.

Goldschmidt, Friedrich. *Kunstlerische Waffengravuren Ferlacher Meister*. Auflage, Germany: Journal-Verlag Schwend, 1977. German text; great photographs of German engraving.

Greener, W. W. *Modern Breechloader*. London, England: Cassel, Petter and Galpin, 1871. All of Greener's books are excellent references.

———. *Choke Bore Guns*. London, England: Cassel, Petter and Galpin, 1876.

———. *Modern Shotguns*. London, England: Cassel & Company, Ltd., 1888.

———. *The Breech-Loader and How to Use It*. London, England: Cassel & Company, Ltd., 1893.

———. *The Gun (9th ed.)*. New York: Bonanza Books, 1910 (reprint). This book is a standard and well regarded.

Hastings, Macdonald. *English Sporting Guns and Accessories*. London: Ward Lock & Co., Ltd., 1969. A photograph book with limited text.

————. *The Shotgun.* London, England: David and Charles, 1981. A very good book on guns, equipment, and shooting.

Hawker, Col. Peter. *Instructions to Young Sportsmen.* Richmond, Surrey, England : Richmond Pub. Co., Ltd., 1833 (reprint). An interesting historical reference work.

Heather, Purple (pen name). *Something About Guns and Shooting.* London, England: Alexander and Shepherd, 1891. History told as it was being made.

Journee, General. *Tir des Fusils de Chasse.* French text, 1902. A classic on shotgun ballistics and often quoted.

King, Peter. *The Shooting Field.* London, England: Quiller Press Ltd., 1985. A History of the Holland & Holland company.

Lancaster, Charles. *Illustrated Treatise on the Art of Shooting.* London, England: Atkin, Grant & Lang, Ltd., 1889. One of the earliest books on how to shoot and how to pick a shotgun and accessories.

————. *Notes on the Proof of Shotguns and Other Small Arms (4th ed.).* London & Birmingham Proof Houses, 1981. An invaluable reference on proof and proof marks.

Lupi, Gianoberto. *Grandi Fucili da Caccia.* Rome, Italy: Editoriale Olimpia, 1972. Italian text; good photographs.

Marchington, James. *Book of Shotguns.* London, England: Pelham Books, 1984. Types of guns, their performance, and field shooting.

Marshall-Ball, Robin. *Sporting Shotgun.* Hindhead, Surrey, England: Saiga Publishing, 1981. Compares types of guns; field shooting.

Meek, James. *Art of Engraving.* Montezuma, Iowa: Brownell & Son, 1973. A treatise on engraving.

Mills, Desmond and Barnes, Mike. *Amateur Gunsmithing.* Woodbridge, Suffolk, England: Boydell Press, 1986. Good information and pictures of shotgun internals.

Nobili, Marco. *Fucili D'Autore.* Rome, Italy: Il Volo sri, 1991 (2nd ed. with English text). This is a poor translation, but it has good photos and information on Italian guns.

————. *Il Grande Libro Delle Incisioni.* Rome, Italy: Il Volo sri, 1992. Incredible photographs of Italian engraving.

Oberfell, Dr. George G. and Thompson, Charles E. *Mysteries of Shotgun Patterns.* Stillwater, Oklahoma: Oklahoma State University Press, 1960. Shotgun ballistics, a mathematical, technical viewpoint.

Payne-Gallwey, Sir Ralph. *Letters to Young Shooters—Volume I–1890, Volume II–1894, Volume III–1896*. London, England: Longmans, Green & Co. Wonderful historical references; colorful and informative.

Pollard, Hugh. *Shot-Guns*. London, England: Pitman & Sons, Ltd., 1923. Well written and informative.

Purdey, James & Sons. *Purdey Guns*, London, England: James Purdey & Sons, 1929. Instruction book for Purdey guns.

Spearing, G. N. *Craft of the Gunsmith*. Poole, Dorset, England: Blandford Press, 1986. The life and work of a gunsmith.

Taylor, John. *African Rifles and Cartridges*. Long Beach, CA: Safari Press, 1994. A standard for double rifles and cartridges.

———. *Big Game and Big-Game Rifles*. Long Beach, CA: Safari Press, 1993. More good text on this subject.

Teasdale-Buckell, G. T. *Experts on Guns and Shooting*. London, England: Sampson Low, Marston & Co., 1900 (reprint). Interesting information about gunmakers.

Thomas, Gough. *Shotguns and Cartridges for Game and Clays*. London, England: A & C Black, Ltd., 1963. The Gough Thomas books are essentially a compilation of his magazine articles taken from *The Shooting Times*.

———. *Gough Thomas's Gun Book*. London, England: A & C Black, Ltd., 1969.

———. *Gough Thomas's Second Gun Book*. London, England: A & C Black, Ltd., 1971.

———. *Shooting Facts and Fancies*. London, England: A & C Black, Ltd., 1978.

Truesdell, S. R. *The Rifle*. Long Beach, CA: Safari Press, 1992. Basic information on double rifles and cartridges.

"20-Bore" (pen name). *Practical Hints on Shooting*. London, England: Kegal Paul, Trench & Co., 1887. Guns and paraphernalia and how to shoot game.

Wallack, L. R. *American Shotgun Design and Performance*. New York: Winchester Press, 1977. Guns and ballistics from the American viewpoint.

Walsh, J. H. *Modern Sportman's Gun and Rifle, Volume I*, 1882. Excellent and informative general text by the editor of *The Field*.

Zutz, D. *Double Shotgun*. New York: Winchester Press, 1978. Information on double guns made worldwide.

Selected Annotated Bibliography

Part II – Shooting with Consistency

Selected Annotated Bibliography
Part II - Shooting with Consistency

Baekeland, George. *Gunner's Guide*. New York: Macmillan, 1943. Discussion of guns, cartridges, and how to shoot.

Blue Rock (pen name). *Pigeon Shooting*. New York: Shooting and Fishing Publishing Co., 1896. Good presentation on perhaps the most difficult of all shotgunning.

Bogardus, Adam. *Field, Cover and Trap Shooting*. New York: (self-published), 1878. Shooting tips from one of history's greatest shots.

Brander, Michael. *Game Shot's Vade Mecum*. London, England: Adam & Charles Black, 1965. Shotguns and shooting, illustrated with good line drawings.

Brindle, John. *Shotgun Shooting: Techniques and Technology*. Hindhead, Surrey, England: Nimrod Book Services, 1984. Guns and shooting, illustrated with numerous line drawings.

Brister, Bob. *Shotgunning — the Art and the Science*. New York: Winchester Press, 1976. The most current American book on the technical aspects of shooting.

Bumstead, John. *On the Wing*. New York: Happy Hours Company, 1869. Interesting reading.

Churchill, Robert. *How to Shoot*. London, England: Geoffrey Bles, 1925. A treatise on the Churchill method.

Cradock, Chris. *A Manual on Clay Shooting*. London, England: Batsford Ltd, 1983. Good tips from a famous shooter and coach.

Davies, Ken. *The Better Shot*. London, England: Quiller Press, 1992. Excellent book with tips from perhaps the world's most famous instructor.

Dougall, James. *Shooting*. London, England: Samson Low, Marston, Low & Searle, 1875. Guns and shooting by a great gunmaker.

East Sussex (pen name). *The Shot Gun and Its Uses*. London, England: Simpkin, Marshall, Hamilton, Kent & Co., Ltd., 1914. Discussion of guns and equipment and game shooting.

Etchen, Fred. *Common Sense Shotgun Shooting*. Huntington, West Virginia: Standard Publications, Inc., 1946. An interesting book by one of America's greatest coaches.

Hastings, Macdonald. *Game Shooting.* London, England: Michael Joseph, 1955. Additional viewpoints on the Churchill system.

Hearn, Arthur. *Shooting and Gunfitting.* London, England: Herbert Jenkins Limited, 1942. A good book on gunfitting and the proper way to shoot.

Kemp, Michael. *Shooting Game.* London, England: Adam & Charles Black, 1972. A well-written book on game shooting.

Lancaster, Charles. *The Art of Shooting.* London, England: Atkin, Grant & Lang, Ltd., 1889. One of the first books on how to shoot, and how to pick a shotgun and accessories.

Leffingwell, William. *Art of Wing Shooting.* New York: Arno Press, 1890 (reprint). Excellent early book on shooting.

Long, W. H. T. *The Gun in the Field.* London, England: Robert Hale Ltd., 1948. A collection of field shooting articles from *The Field.*

Marksman (pen name). *The Dead Shot.* New York: The American News Co., 1873. An early book on gun selection and how to shoot.

Montague, Andrew. *Successful Shotgun Shooting.* New York: Winchester Press, 1971. Well done and informative.

Moore, H. Gordon. *Trigger Pullers.* Richmond, Virginia: Dietz Press, 1976. A collection of gun and shooting articles from *Field and Stream.*

No Author given. *Notes on Shooting, 9th ed.* London, England: Curtis's & Harvey, 1915. An informative book written by an expert and published by a powder company.

Parker, Eric. *Elements of Shooting.* London, England: The Field Press Ltd., 1924. A reference book primarily on field shooting.

Paulet, Michael. *Shooting from Scratch.* London, England: Buchan & Enright, 1987. A book on both field and target guns and shooting.

Payne-Gallwey, Sir Ralph. *High Pheasants in Theory and in Practice.* London, England: Longmans, Green & Co., 1913. A classic analysis of shooting high birds.

Purdey, T. D. S. and Purdey, Capt. J. A. *The Shotgun.* London, England: Adams & Charles Black, 1936. Shotguns and field shooting in Britain.

Rastelli, Giorgio. *Il Tiro di Pedana al Volatili.* Rome, Italy: Editoriale Olimpia, 1970. Italian text; a treatise on live pigeon shooting.

Rose, Michael. *Eley Book of Shooting Technique*. London, England: Chancerel, 1978. Instructional illustrations and photographs from a fine teacher.

Smith, Lawrence. *Shotgun Psychology*. New York: Scribners & Sons, 1938. An excellent book on shooting.

Stanbury, Percy and Carlisle, G. L. *Shotgun Marksmanship*. London, England: Barry & Jenkins, 1962. A classic book on the famous Stanbury method.

Uquillas Sota, Humberto. *Polvora Y Perdigones*. Mexico City, Mexico: (self-published), 1982. Spanish text; a basic shooting reference.

Yardley, Michael. *Gunfitting*. London, England: Sportsman's Press, 1993. A good treatise on the subject.